The Things Wealthy People Do

JUSTINE EHIWARIO

TABLE OF CONTENTS

SUMMARY

The Things Wealthy People Do

By Justine Ehiwario

Wealth is not a matter of luck—it is the result of intentional actions, disciplined habits, and a success-driven mindset. *The Things Rich People Do* unveils the financial principles, strategies, and decision-making processes that set the wealthy apart from the rest. Drawing insights from *The Unstoppable Road to Wealth Creation*, this book provides a practical roadmap to achieving financial success and sustaining long-term prosperity.

Inside, you will discover:

✅ The mindset transformations necessary to attract and maintain wealth

✅ How to break free from financial limitations and develop a prosperity-driven outlook

✅ The money habits and financial strategies that foster long-term success

✅ The power of strategic relationships and leveraging networks for wealth creation

✅ The importance of multiple income streams, wise investments, and calculated risks

Success with money isn't accidental—it is cultivated through knowledge, persistence, and the right financial moves. Whether you are an aspiring entrepreneur, a career professional, or someone looking to break free from financial struggles, *The Things Rich People Do* equips you with the tools to build and sustain wealth.

Are you ready to take control of your financial destiny? The journey to lasting prosperity starts now!

ACKNOWLEDGMENTS

Writing *The Things Rich People Do* has been an incredible journey, and I am deeply grateful to those who have supported and inspired me along the way.

First and foremost, I give thanks to God for the wisdom, strength, and vision to bring this book to life. Without divine guidance, none of this would have been possible.

To my beloved wife, Odion, and my wonderful children, Justine, Jason, and Jolene—your love, encouragement, and patience have been my greatest motivation. Your belief in me fuels my determination to keep pushing forward.

To my sweet mother, thank you for your selfless nurturing. You shall enjoy the fruits of your labour of love—may the Lord continue to be your strength.

To my brother, Michael, and my beloved siblings, your care and support throughout the years remain dear to me. Your presence in my life has shaped me in ways I deeply appreciate.

To my mentors, business associates, and friends, your invaluable insights and experiences have played a significant role in shaping my journey. Your success stories and wisdom have enriched these pages.

To my readers and supporters, your engagement and feedback continue to inspire me. I hope this book empowers you to take control of your financial future and build lasting wealth.

Finally, to everyone pursuing financial freedom and success, may this book serve as a guiding light on your journey to prosperity.

With gratitude,
Justine Ehiwario

DISCLAIMER

The content in *The Things Rich People Do* is intended for informational and educational purposes only. While every effort has been made to provide accurate and valuable insights, the author and publisher make no guarantees regarding specific financial outcomes from applying the strategies discussed.

This book does not serve as financial, investment, legal, or tax advice. Readers are encouraged to conduct independent research and seek guidance from qualified professionals before making financial or investment decisions. The principles shared are based on personal experiences, research, and observations, but results may vary for each individual.

The author and publisher are not responsible for any financial losses, consequences, or outcomes resulting from the application of the information in this book. Achieving financial success requires individual responsibility, effort, and informed decision-making.

By reading this book, you acknowledge that your financial choices are your own and that the author and publisher bear no liability for any actions taken based on its content.

PART 1:

THE WEALTH MINDSET

CHAPTER 1: THINKING LIKE THE WEALTHY- UNDERSTANDING THE PSYCHOLOGY OF WEALTH

Introduction

Wealth is more than just money; it is a mindset that shapes decisions, habits, and actions. Many aspire to financial success, yet only a select few attain it. The key difference between the wealthy and the average person lies in their perception of money, opportunities, and growth. As Napoleon Hill famously stated in *Think and Grow Rich*, "Whatever the mind can conceive and believe, it can achieve."

In *The Unstoppable Road to Wealth Creation*, I emphasized that financial success begins in the mind before it materializes in reality. This chapter delves into the unique ways the wealthy think and how adopting a similar mindset can pave the way for financial prosperity.

The Wealthy Embrace Abundance Over Scarcity

Many people operate with a scarcity mindset, fearing that resources are limited and that wealth accumulation comes at the expense of others. This perspective fosters fear, risk aversion, and limited ambition. In contrast, the wealthy embrace an abundance mindset, recognizing limitless opportunities and believing in the expansive nature of wealth.

As highlighted in *The Unstoppable Road to Wealth Creation*, the world thrives on expansion, not limitation. Wealth grows through value creation. For instance, Warren Buffett, one of the world's most successful investors, has consistently emphasized long-term value creation. He once said, "The more you learn, the more you earn." This statement embodies an abundant mindset—wealth is not about taking, but about creating.

How to Cultivate an Abundance Mindset:

1. Recognize that opportunities are limitless—seek ways to add value instead of fearing competition.
2. Invest in self-development—read books, take courses, and expand your knowledge.
3. Surround yourself with successful individuals—your network greatly influences your financial success.

Wealthy Individuals View Problems as Opportunities

While most people see challenges as obstacles, the wealthy perceive them as stepping stones to success. Some of the greatest fortunes have been built by those who identified problems and provided innovative solutions.

Take Elon Musk, for example. Rather than viewing the challenges of space travel and electric vehicles as insurmountable, he saw them as opportunities for groundbreaking advancements. His ventures, including Tesla and SpaceX, are driven by a mindset that sees problems as catalysts for progress.

As discussed in *The Unstoppable Road to Wealth Creation*, every major breakthrough results from someone daring to solve a problem others overlook. By training yourself to view challenges as opportunities, you open doors to financial success that many fail to recognize.

Actionable Steps:

- View everyday challenges as opportunities for innovation.
- Develop problem-solving skills instead of avoiding difficulties.
- Embrace setbacks as learning experiences.

The Wealthy Prioritize Long-Term Gains Over Short-Term Gratification

A fundamental difference between the wealthy and the average person is their approach to time and gratification. Many seek immediate pleasure, spending on luxuries and unnecessary expenses, while avoiding delayed rewards. The wealthy, however, exercise patience and prioritize long-term growth.

Jeff Bezos, the founder of Amazon, exemplified this mindset by reinvesting profits back into the company for years before it became a trillion-dollar enterprise. His approach was not about making quick money but about building sustainable wealth.

In *The Unstoppable Road to Wealth Creation*, I highlighted that real wealth is built by those who delay gratification and allow investments to compound over time. The ability to prioritize long-term success over short-term pleasure is crucial for financial growth.

How to Develop a Long-Term Mindset:

1. Invest instead of spend—prioritize assets over liabilities.
2. Think years ahead—make decisions that benefit your future, not just the present.
3. Develop patience—understand that wealth-building is a marathon, not a sprint.

Wealthy People Commit to Lifelong Learning

"The illiterate of the 21st century will not be those who cannot read and write, but those who cannot learn, unlearn, and relearn." – Alvin Toffler

Wealthy individuals are committed to continuous learning. They read books, attend seminars, network with successful people, and consistently seek personal growth. Bill Gates, despite being one of the richest individuals in the world, reads about 50 books per year, recognizing that knowledge compounds over time.

In *The Unstoppable Road to Wealth Creation*, I emphasized that continuous learning accelerates wealth-building. Stagnation is the enemy of financial growth, and those who do not expand their knowledge risk falling behind.

What You Can Do:

- Read daily—books like *Rich Dad Poor Dad* by Robert Kiyosaki and *The Millionaire Next Door* by Thomas Stanley offer valuable insights.
- Invest in skills—learning high-income skills such as sales, investing, or digital marketing can significantly boost your earning potential.
- Seek mentorship—learning from successful individuals can fast-track your journey.

Wealthy People Control Their Emotions Around Money

Emotional spending, fear-driven decisions, and impulsive financial choices often hinder wealth-building. The wealthy, however, practice emotional discipline when it comes to money.

Warren Buffett wisely advises, "If you cannot control your emotions, you cannot control your money." Emotional decision-making leads to unnecessary spending, poor investments, and financial instability.

Successful individuals adopt a rational, strategic approach to their finances.

In *The Unstoppable Road to Wealth Creation*, I stressed that wealthy individuals think logically about money rather than letting emotions dictate their financial choices. They create structured plans for saving, investing, and spending that align with their long-term goals.

How to Practice Emotional Discipline:

1. Set a budget and adhere to it—avoid impulsive purchases.
2. Base investment decisions on research, not emotions or market hype.
3. View money as a tool for value creation rather than just for consumption.

Conclusion: Developing the Wealth Mindset

Achieving financial success is not a matter of luck or privilege but of mindset, discipline, and strategic thinking. If you aspire to wealth, you must first cultivate the mindset of the wealthy.

Key Takeaways:

✅ Shift from a scarcity mindset to an abundance mindset.

✅ View problems as opportunities for growth and innovation.

✅ Prioritize long-term wealth over short-term gratification.

✅ Commit to continuous learning and self-improvement.

✅ Control emotions around money and make rational financial choices.

By internalizing these principles, you lay the foundation for financial success. In the next chapter, we will explore the power of vision and goal-setting and how they drive the wealthy toward their ambitions and financial freedom.

CHAPTER 2: THE POWER OF VISION AND GOAL SETTING – HOW THE RICH PLAN FOR SUCCESS

Introduction

Wealth is never an accident. Every financially successful individual has a well-defined vision and a strategic plan to achieve their goals. The wealthy do not depend on luck; they create clear roadmaps for their future, ensuring that every action they take aligns with their ultimate aspirations. As Tony Robbins puts it, "Setting goals is the first step in turning the invisible into the visible."

In *The Unstoppable Road to Wealth Creation*, I stressed that without a clear vision, financial success remains elusive. This chapter will explore how the wealthy use vision and goal-setting as essential tools to build, sustain, and grow their wealth.

The Wealthy Have a Clear Vision

Successful individuals recognize that having a compelling vision fosters motivation, resilience, and purpose. A strong vision provides direction and clarity, allowing them to overcome obstacles without losing focus.

Why Vision Matters:

1. **It Creates Purpose** – A strong financial goal keeps you committed, even in difficult times.
2. **It Shapes Decision-Making** – Knowing where you want to be in 10, 20, or 30 years helps you make choices that align with your long-term aspirations.
3. **It Fuels Motivation** – A clear vision keeps you inspired and pushes you to take consistent action.

Take Jeff Bezos, for example. His vision for Amazon was to create an effortless and customer-centric online shopping experience. This guiding vision helped him transform a small online bookstore into a trillion-dollar empire.

How to Develop Your Wealth Vision:

- Define what financial success means to you.
- Visualize your ideal future, including your dream lifestyle, investments, and business ventures.
- Write down your vision, making it specific, measurable, and time-bound.

Goal-Setting: The Blueprint for Wealth

Having a vision is just the beginning; the real transformation happens when you break it down into actionable goals. The wealthy are meticulous about setting SMART goals—Specific, Measurable, Achievable, Relevant, and Time-bound.

The SMART Goal Framework:

1. **Specific** – Clearly define what you want to achieve.
2. **Measurable** – Track progress with tangible milestones.
3. **Achievable** – Set realistic yet challenging goals.
4. **Relevant** – Ensure your goals align with your long-term vision.
5. **Time-bound** – Establish deadlines to create a sense of urgency.

In *The Unstoppable Road to Wealth Creation*, I emphasized that vague goals lead to vague results. Financial success requires setting precise and strategic objectives.

Examples of Wealth-Oriented Goals:

- **Short-Term Goals (1-5 years):** Save £50,000, start investing in the stock market, or purchase rental property.
- **Mid-Term Goals (5-10 years):** Expand your business, achieve financial independence, or build a diversified investment portfolio.
- **Long-Term Goals (10+ years):** Generate passive income streams, create generational wealth, or establish philanthropic initiatives.

The Power of Writing Down Goals

Research indicates that individuals who write down their goals are 42% more likely to achieve them. Recording your goals solidifies them and serves as a constant reminder of what you are striving for.

Actionable Steps:

- Keep a wealth journal and write down your financial goals.
- Review your goals daily to reinforce commitment.
- Adjust your goals as necessary, but remain consistent in execution.

The Wealthy Use Visualization Techniques

Visualization is a powerful tool that the wealthy use to bring their goals to life. By mentally picturing their desired outcomes, they program their subconscious minds for success.

How to Use Visualization:

1. **Create a Vision Board** – Use images and quotes that represent your financial goals.
2. **Practice Mental Rehearsal** – Spend a few minutes each day visualizing yourself achieving success.
3. **Affirm Success** – Repeat positive affirmations that reinforce your financial ambitions.

Oprah Winfrey attributes much of her success to visualization. She famously said, "Create the highest, grandest vision possible for your life, because you become what you believe."

Setting Wealth Routines and Daily Habits

The wealthy do not just set goals; they develop daily habits that drive them toward success. They understand that wealth accumulation is a result of consistent effort rather than occasional action.

Wealth-Building Habits:

- **Start the Day with a Success Routine** – Meditate, exercise, and read financial literature.
- **Track Your Progress** – Use financial tracking apps or journals to monitor growth.
- **Surround Yourself with Successful Individuals** – Network with like-minded people who inspire you.
- **Invest Consistently** – Automate investments to ensure steady financial growth.

As discussed in *The Unstoppable Road to Wealth Creation*, financial success is not about luck but about cultivating daily habits that align with wealth-building strategies.

The Importance of Accountability

Wealthy individuals hold themselves accountable for their financial progress. They track their achievements, learn from failures, and adjust their strategies as needed.

Ways to Stay Accountable:

- Find a mentor or accountability partner.
- Join a mastermind group focused on financial success.
- Conduct monthly progress reviews and adjust strategies accordingly.

Overcoming Obstacles in Goal-Setting

Not every goal will be easy to achieve, but the wealthy understand that challenges are stepping stones to success. When faced with obstacles, they re-strategize and push forward instead of giving up.

How to Overcome Challenges:

1. **Stay Flexible** – Adapt your goals to changing circumstances without abandoning them.
2. **Learn from Mistakes** – Treat failures as lessons rather than setbacks.
3. **Keep the Bigger Picture in Mind** – Focus on long-term success over temporary difficulties.

Conclusion: Planning for Wealth with Precision

The power of vision and goal-setting is undeniable. Wealthy individuals do not leave financial success to chance; they create a strategic roadmap and follow it diligently.

Key Takeaways:

✅ Develop a clear vision for your financial future.
✅ Set SMART goals that align with your vision.
✅ Write down your goals and visualize success daily.
✅ Build daily habits that support wealth creation.
✅ Stay accountable and adjust strategies when needed.

By mastering the art of vision and goal-setting, you take control of your financial destiny. In the next chapter, we will explore how developing unshakable discipline separates the wealthy from the rest.

CHAPTER 3: BUILDING UNSHAKABLE DISCIPLINE – THE HABITS THAT DISTINGUISH THE WEALTHY

Introduction

Discipline is the cornerstone of financial success. While having a vision and setting goals create direction, discipline is what bridges the gap between ambition and achievement. Wealthy individuals do not depend on fleeting bursts of motivation; instead, they cultivate strong discipline that ensures consistent progress toward their financial goals.

In *The Unstoppable Road to Wealth Creation*, I emphasized that financial success is not merely about how much one earns, but how consistently one applies principles of wealth-building. This chapter delves into the core habits and mindset shifts that separate the financially disciplined from those who struggle to sustain wealth.

Discipline as a Pathway to Financial Freedom

Discipline is often perceived as a restrictive force, but in reality, it is the key to financial freedom. It ensures that actions align with long-term financial objectives and prevents impulsive decisions from undermining progress.

As Jim Rohn once said, *"Discipline is the bridge between goals and accomplishment."* This chapter will explore how disciplined habits create financial success and how you can develop them to transform your wealth trajectory.

Why Discipline is Crucial:

1. **Ensures Consistency** – Wealth is accumulated through continuous effort and strategic financial decisions.
2. **Prevents Impulse Spending** – The ability to delay gratification is a defining trait of the wealthy.
3. **Encourages Resilience** – Disciplined individuals remain steadfast through financial setbacks and economic fluctuations.
4. **Drives Long-Term Success** – Building wealth is a gradual process, and discipline keeps you focused on the journey.

Warren Buffett wisely stated, "We don't have to be smarter than the rest. We have to be more disciplined than the rest." This principle is fundamental to wealth creation.

The Essential Habits of the Financially Disciplined

Wealthy individuals follow structured habits that reinforce financial discipline. These habits are intentional and unwavering.

1. Practicing Self-Control in Financial Decisions

A key distinction between the wealthy and the average person is their ability to resist impulsive financial decisions. Instead of yielding to immediate desires, they make calculated choices.

Practical Steps:

- Implement a **24-hour rule** before making significant purchases to curb impulse spending.
- Maintain a **strict budget** and track every dollar or pound spent.
- Avoid **lifestyle inflation**—increased earnings should be used for wealth-building rather than unnecessary expenditures.

2. Establishing Structured Financial Routines

Wealthy individuals maintain financial routines that reinforce discipline and ensure that they stay aligned with their wealth-building goals.

Daily Financial Habits:

- Review financial goals each morning to maintain focus.
- Track income and expenses to prevent financial mismanagement.
- Make consistent investments to secure long-term growth.

3. Developing a Strong Work Ethic

Discipline extends beyond financial habits to the approach taken toward work, business, and investment decisions. Wealthy individuals understand that success is built on perseverance and diligence.

Ways to Strengthen Work Ethic:

- Set daily productivity goals to ensure purposeful effort.
- Eliminate distractions and maintain a focused work environment.

- Stay committed even in challenging times—persistence is key.

Financial Education as a Tool for Discipline

Many people fail financially not due to lack of opportunities but because they lack financial literacy. The wealthy prioritize ongoing education in money management, investment strategies, and economic trends.

Strategies for Continuous Learning:

- Read books and materials on wealth-building and investing.
- Attend financial seminars and workshops.
- Keep track of market trends and economic developments.
- Surround yourself with financially savvy and disciplined individuals.

Robert Kiyosaki, author of *Rich Dad Poor Dad*, said, "The single most powerful asset we all have is our mind. If it is trained well, it can create enormous wealth."

Strengthening Financial Discipline

Like a muscle, discipline grows stronger with consistent effort. Implementing these strategies will help maintain financial discipline and sustain wealth.

1. Automating Wealth-Building Processes

To minimize the risk of poor financial decisions, the wealthy rely on automated financial systems.

Examples of Automated Systems:

- **Automatic savings contributions** ensure consistent savings before discretionary spending.

- **Scheduled investment allocations** create a habit of long-term wealth accumulation.
- **Recurring debt payments** prevent late fees and strengthen creditworthiness.

2. Holding Oneself Accountable

Accountability plays a significant role in sustaining financial discipline. The wealthy employ various strategies to remain on track.

Ways to Stay Accountable:

- Partner with a **mentor or financial accountability partner**.
- Join **financial mastermind groups** to gain insights and encouragement.
- Set **financial milestones** and conduct monthly progress evaluations.

3. Building Mental Resilience

Wealth-building is not free of challenges. The financially disciplined differentiate themselves through their ability to handle setbacks effectively.

How to Develop Resilience:

- View failures as learning opportunities rather than obstacles.
- Adapt strategies when necessary but remain committed to goals.
- Celebrate small financial victories to maintain motivation.

As highlighted in *The Unstoppable Road to Wealth Creation*, resilience and discipline go hand in hand. The stronger your financial discipline, the more resilient you become in the face of challenges.

Conclusion: The Power of Discipline in Achieving Wealth

Financial discipline is the silent force behind every successful wealth journey. It determines whether one achieves financial freedom or remains caught in the cycle of financial struggle.

Key Takeaways:

✅ Consistency is the foundation of wealth-building success.

✅ Delaying gratification is a fundamental principle of financial discipline.

✅ Structured financial habits lead to long-term wealth accumulation.

✅ Continuous financial education enhances decision-making and discipline.

✅ Accountability and resilience keep you committed to long-term financial goals.

By fostering unwavering financial discipline, you position yourself alongside the world's most financially successful individuals. In the next chapter, we will explore how to overcome limiting beliefs and break free from poverty mindsets.

CHAPTER 4: OVERCOMING LIMITING BELIEFS – BREAKING FREE FROM POVERTY MINDSETS

Introduction

Our beliefs shape our reality, and nowhere is this truer than in financial success. Many remain trapped in financial struggles not due to a lack of opportunity but because of deep-seated limiting beliefs. These thoughts, often ingrained from childhood or societal conditioning, create a mental barrier that restricts financial progress.

Wealthy individuals understand that financial success starts with the right mindset. As I emphasized in *The Unstoppable Road to Wealth Creation*, your thoughts influence your actions, and your actions determine your financial destiny. This chapter explores how to identify and overcome limiting beliefs that hinder wealth accumulation, drawing from the experiences of successful individuals and key insights from my personal journey.

Understanding Limiting Beliefs and Their Impact

Limiting beliefs are assumptions that restrict a person's potential. These subconscious thoughts create a self-fulfilling cycle where individuals unknowingly sabotage their financial success.

Common Limiting Beliefs About Wealth:

- **"Money is the root of all evil."** This belief creates guilt around wealth accumulation, leading to self-sabotage.
- **"I'm not good with money."** Such a mindset discourages financial literacy and responsible money management.
- **"Wealth is only for the lucky or privileged."** This notion prevents people from actively working toward financial success.
- **"I must work harder, not smarter, to be rich."** Hard work is essential, but strategic planning and leveraging opportunities are crucial.
- **"If I become wealthy, I will lose my friends or family will take advantage of me."** Fear of isolation can prevent financial growth.

Each of these beliefs hinders people from taking the necessary actions to build wealth. Recognizing and challenging them is the first step toward financial freedom.

How Wealthy Individuals Think Differently

The wealthy develop empowering beliefs that support their financial growth. In *The Unstoppable Road to Wealth Creation*, I highlighted the importance of shifting from a scarcity mindset to an abundance mindset. Here's how successful individuals think:

Wealth-Building Mindsets:

- **"Money is a tool for impact and freedom."** Wealth allows people to create opportunities and improve lives.
- **"Financial skills can be learned."** Successful individuals continuously educate themselves on wealth management.
- **"Opportunities for wealth are everywhere."** Instead of seeing obstacles, they focus on possibilities.
- **"Smart work and strategic investments lead to financial growth."** Wealth is built through leveraging knowledge, networking, and systems.
- **"I attract abundance by providing value."** Wealth follows those who solve problems and serve others effectively.

By adopting these perspectives, anyone can unlock their full financial potential.

Steps to Overcome Limiting Beliefs

Changing deeply rooted beliefs requires conscious effort and repeated action. The following steps help rewire the mindset for financial success.

1. Identifying Negative Financial Beliefs

Acknowledge the limiting beliefs that shape your financial behaviours. Pay attention to thoughts that arise when discussing or making financial decisions.

Action Steps:

- Write down your beliefs about money and wealth.
- Analyse whether these beliefs empower or restrict you.
- Challenge negative beliefs by questioning their validity.

2. Replacing Limiting Beliefs with Empowering Ones

Once financial mindset blocks are recognized, replace them with positive affirmations and constructive perspectives.

Action Steps:

- Reframe **"I'm bad with money"** to **"I am learning to manage my finances wisely."**
- Instead of thinking **"Money is evil,"** affirm **"Money allows me to create a positive impact."**
- Surround yourself with financial success stories that reinforce abundance thinking.

3. Practicing Daily Wealth Affirmations

Affirmations help reprogram the subconscious mind. When repeated consistently, they reshape financial beliefs and habits.

Examples of Wealth Affirmations:

- "I attract financial abundance effortlessly."
- "I am in control of my financial destiny."
- "Money flows to me in expected and unexpected ways."
- "I am worthy of wealth and prosperity."

4. Investing in Financial Education

Lack of financial literacy reinforces limiting beliefs. Actively learning about money management builds confidence in handling finances.

Ways to Improve Financial Knowledge:

- Read books and articles on personal finance and wealth-building.
- Attend financial workshops and seminars.
- Follow successful entrepreneurs and financial experts.

- Take online courses on investing and money management.

5. Surrounding Yourself with Wealth-Minded Individuals

Your environment shapes your beliefs. Engaging with successful and financially literate individuals fosters a wealth mindset.

Action Steps:

- Join mastermind groups or entrepreneurial networks.
- Seek mentorship from successful individuals.
- Limit interactions with people who reinforce financial negativity.

6. Taking Consistent Action Towards Financial Growth

Mindset shifts alone are not enough; action must follow belief. Implement financial strategies that align with your new perspective.

Practical Actions:

- Start budgeting and tracking expenses.
- Set financial goals and break them into achievable steps.
- Create multiple income streams and explore investment opportunities.
- Develop long-term financial plans to ensure sustained growth.

Breaking the Cycle of Poverty Mindsets

Many people are raised in environments where scarcity thinking is prevalent. However, escaping this cycle is possible through conscious efforts.

Strategies to Break Free:

- Challenge inherited financial beliefs by questioning their accuracy.
- Expose yourself to success stories that prove wealth-building is possible.
- Develop resilience to setbacks and view failures as learning experiences.
- Commit to lifelong learning in financial literacy and wealth-building.

Conclusion: Rewiring Your Mind for Wealth

Financial success is not just about external actions but also about internal transformation. As I emphasized in *The Unstoppable Road to Wealth Creation*, overcoming limiting beliefs is a critical step toward financial freedom. By shifting your mindset, educating yourself, and surrounding yourself with positive influences, you can break free from poverty thinking and create lasting financial abundance.

Key Takeaways:

✅ Your beliefs about money shape your financial reality.

✅ Identifying and challenging limiting beliefs is crucial for wealth-building.

✅ Wealthy individuals cultivate empowering mindsets that attract abundance.

✅ Continuous financial education and positive influences reinforce a prosperity mindset.

✅ Consistent action, combined with the right beliefs, leads to financial freedom.

In the next chapter, we will explore the power of strategic networking and how building the right relationships can accelerate your path to wealth.

CHAPTER 5: MASTERING FINANCIAL INTELLIGENCE – LEARNING HOW MONEY WORKS

Introduction

Wealthy individuals don't just earn money—they excel at managing it. Financial intelligence is the key factor that separates those who struggle with money from those who accumulate lasting wealth. Robert Kiyosaki, in *Rich Dad Poor Dad*, emphasizes the importance of financial literacy, stating that it is more crucial than simply earning money. Without financial intelligence, wealth can be quickly lost, but with it, wealth can be multiplied and preserved.

In *The Unstoppable Road to Wealth Creation*, I explained that understanding how money works is fundamental to financial success. This chapter will explore the principles followed by the financially intelligent, how they implement them, and how you can apply these principles to build and protect your wealth.

The Wealthy See Money as a Tool

Money is not just for spending; it is a tool for creating wealth. Financially savvy individuals view money as a way to create opportunities, rather than simply a resource to consume.

Key Differences in Money Management Between the Wealthy and the Poor:

1. **The Wealthy Make Money Work for Them** – They invest in assets that generate passive income.
2. **The Poor Work for Money** – They rely on earned income without leveraging investments.
3. **The Wealthy Understand Delayed Gratification** – They reinvest their earnings instead of spending impulsively.
4. **The Poor Prioritize Instant Gratification** – They spend immediately, often living paycheck to paycheck.

"The rich invest in time, while the poor invest in money." – Robert Kiyosaki

Consider the example of two individuals: John and Peter. John has a high-paying job but spends most of his income on luxury items, while Peter, with a more modest salary, invests part of his earnings in stocks, real estate, and businesses. Over time, Peter's wealth grows, while John remains financially stagnant. This illustrates the power of financial intelligence.

Key Components of Financial Intelligence

To develop financial intelligence, you need to master the following:

1. **Understanding Cash Flow** The wealthy focus on managing cash flow by ensuring their income exceeds expenses, and a portion is reinvested to generate additional income.

Actionable Steps:

- Create a personal cash flow statement to track income, savings, investments, and expenses.
- Aim for a positive cash flow, where your assets generate more income than your liabilities take away.

"Money is a terrible master but an excellent servant." – P.T. Barnum

2. **Differentiating Between Assets and Liabilities As Kiyosaki** famously says, "The rich buy assets, while the poor and middle class buy liabilities, believing they are assets."

Examples:

- **Assets:** Stocks, rental properties, businesses, intellectual property.
- **Liabilities:** Expensive cars, high-interest loans, excessive credit card debt.

Actionable Steps:

- Conduct an audit of your assets and liabilities, eliminating unnecessary liabilities while focusing on acquiring income-generating assets.

"Don't work for money. Make it work for you." – Robert Kiyosaki

3. **The Power of Wise Investment** The wealthy understand that saving alone is not enough; investing is crucial for financial growth.

Common Investment Strategies:

- **Stock Market Investments:** Diversifying portfolios with long-term assets.
- **Real Estate Investments:** Acquiring rental properties to generate passive income.

- **Entrepreneurial Ventures:** Building businesses that yield long-term revenue.

Scenario: Sarah started investing £200 per month in a diversified index fund at 25. By 50, her investments had grown significantly. Her friend Tom, who began investing at 40, struggled to catch up. The lesson here is that the earlier you start investing, the better.

"The stock market is filled with individuals who know the price of everything, but the value of nothing." – Philip Fisher

4. **Using Debt for Growth** The wealthy use debt strategically to create wealth, rather than avoiding it.

Types of Debt:

- **Bad Debt:** High-interest credit card debt, car loans, and unnecessary loans.
- **Good Debt:** Loans for acquiring rental properties, business expansion, or funding investments that appreciate over time.

Example: Mark took a loan to invest in an apartment complex. The rental income covered the mortgage, and within 10 years, he fully owned the property, generating steady income. In contrast, his friend James took a car loan, which only resulted in depreciation and debt after 10 years.

"You must gain control over your money or the lack of it will forever control you." – Dave Ramsey

5. **Understanding Taxes and Legal Structures** The wealthy understand how taxes impact wealth and use legal structures like trusts and corporations to protect their assets.

Strategies:

- Utilize tax-efficient accounts (e.g., ISAs, Roth IRAs).
- Invest in tax-efficient assets.
- Work with financial advisors for strategic tax planning.

Building Financial Intelligence Daily

Actionable Steps to Develop Financial Intelligence:

1. Continuously educate yourself—read books, attend seminars, and follow financial experts.
2. Regularly budget and plan your finances—monitor expenses, set savings goals, and track your progress.
3. Invest in financial tools—use software to track investments and manage money.
4. Surround yourself with wealth-conscious individuals—your financial circle shapes your habits.
5. Take action, even with small investments—the best way to learn is by doing.

Conclusion: Becoming Financially Intelligent

Mastering financial intelligence distinguishes those who struggle with money from those who thrive in wealth. Wealthy individuals don't rely on luck; they understand how money works, make informed decisions, and continually grow their wealth.

Key Takeaways:

✅ Treat money as a tool to create wealth, not just for spending.

✅ Understand cash flow, assets, and liabilities to manage your finances effectively.

✅ Invest in diverse opportunities to generate multiple income streams.

✅ Use good debt strategically to build wealth.

✅ Continuously educate yourself and take action toward financial mastery.

By implementing these principles, you can achieve financial mastery and secure a path to lasting wealth. In the next chapter, we'll explore how the wealthy leverage multiple income streams to ensure financial security and growth.

PART 2:

THE WEALTH BLUEPRINT

CHAPTER 6: CREATING MULTIPLE STREAMS OF INCOME – HOW THE WEALTHY BUILD FINANCIAL SECURITY

Introduction

The wealthy understand that relying on a single income stream is a risky approach. Instead, they diversify their sources of income, ensuring that money flows from multiple channels regardless of economic shifts. As Warren Buffett wisely advises, *"Never depend on a single income. Make investment to create a second source."*

In *The Unstoppable Road to Wealth Creation*, I emphasized that having various streams of income is the key to achieving financial independence. In this chapter, we'll delve into the strategies the wealthy use to create and maintain diverse income sources, ensuring that financial setbacks don't derail their wealth.

Why Multiple Streams of Income Matter

Having multiple income streams offers several key advantages:

1. **Financial Stability** – If one stream decreases, others can help sustain you.
2. **Accelerated Wealth Accumulation** – Multiple streams of income can speed up financial growth.
3. **Freedom and Flexibility** – You are no longer tied to a single employer or business.
4. **Protection During Economic Downturns** – Different income streams act as safety nets when times get tough.
5. **Legacy Building** – Generating multiple sources of income helps build wealth that lasts across generations.

"Do not save what is left after spending, but spend what is left after saving." – Warren Buffett

Imagine two people: Alex, who depends solely on his job, and David, who has a job, rental properties, stock investments, and a side business. When their company announces layoffs, Alex struggles financially, while David remains secure. This scenario underscores why the wealthy prioritize income diversification.

Types of Income Streams the Wealthy Utilize

The wealthy leverage various types of income streams to ensure their financial growth and stability:

Earned Income (Active Income).

This income comes from working, whether through a job or self-employment. While it requires active effort, it is the foundation on which other streams can be built.

Actionable Steps:

- o Maximize your skills to increase your earning potential.
- o Negotiate salaries or look for opportunities for career advancement.

"The best way to predict the future is to create it." – Peter Drucker

Business Income.

Owning a business provides the potential to earn beyond the limits of a traditional job. Entrepreneurs can scale their businesses to generate continuous income.

Actionable Steps:

- o Start a side business in a field you are passionate about or have expertise in.
- o Utilize online platforms like e-commerce, digital products, or freelancing to scale your efforts.

3. Investment Income.

This income comes from investing in stocks, bonds, and real estate that generate returns over time.

Example:
Sarah invests in dividend-paying stocks and receives quarterly pay-outs. Over time, her portfolio grows, providing her with a steady stream of passive income.

Actionable Steps:

- o Start investing early, focusing on long-term growth.
- o Diversify your investment portfolio to manage risk.

"The stock market is a device for transferring money from the impatient to the patient." – Warren Buffett

4. **Rental Income.**

   Owning rental properties provides consistent cash flow and the potential for long-term asset appreciation.

   Example:

   James buys a duplex and rents out one unit while living in the other. The rent covers his mortgage, helping him build equity without added costs.

Actionable Steps:

- Consider real estate investments, such as purchasing rental properties or REITs.
- Focus on locations that will offer profitable returns.

5. **Royalties and Licensing Income.**

   Income from intellectual property like books, patents, or licensing ideas is a powerful passive income source.

   Example:

   Justine writes a book that continues to sell on Amazon, earning him royalties for years with minimal ongoing effort.

Actionable Steps:

- Monetize your expertise by writing books, creating courses, or licensing content.
- If you invent something unique, protect it by filing for patents.

6. **Affiliate and Network Marketing Income.**

   In affiliate marketing, you earn commissions by promoting

others' products. While network marketing can be controversial, it can also be lucrative if done with reputable companies.

Actionable Steps:

- Join affiliate programs like Amazon Associates, ClickBank, or ShareASale.
- Build an audience on social media or YouTube to earn commissions from your recommendations.

7. **Passive Business and Automated Income.**
   Automated income from businesses like dropshipping or digital products requires little ongoing involvement.

   Example:
   Lisa creates an online course on graphic design. Even while she sleeps, students continue to enroll, providing her with passive income.

Actionable Steps:

- Use automation in e-commerce, content creation, and digital marketing.
- Create digital assets like online courses, templates, or membership sites.

"The most important investment you can make is in yourself." – Warren Buffett

How to Create Multiple Income Streams

1. **Start with One Income Source and Expand**
   Begin with what you already have—your job or existing business—and look for strategic ways to expand.
2. **Invest in Income-Producing Assets**
   Prioritize purchasing assets over liabilities to ensure steady income growth.

3. **Leverage Your Skills and Passions**
   Monetize your expertise through consulting, freelancing, or teaching online.

Adopt the Wealthy Mindset

- View money as a tool for investment, not just for spending.
- Be open to learning and adapting to new financial opportunities.

4. **Automate and Scale**
   Once a business or investment proves profitable, automate and scale it to increase revenue without requiring constant effort.

Overcoming Challenges in Income Diversification

Many people hesitate to diversify their income because of fear, lack of knowledge, or perceived risks. However, the wealthy understand that taking calculated risks is essential to achieving financial freedom.

How to Overcome These Challenges:

1. **Lack of Time?** – Start small with low-maintenance sources like stocks or digital products.
2. **Fear of Risk?** – Educate yourself before making investments or starting new ventures.
3. **Not Enough Capital?** – Begin with low-cost opportunities and reinvest profits to expand over time.

"Risk comes from not knowing what you're doing." – Warren Buffett

Conclusion: Build Wealth with Multiple Streams of Income

Diversification is the cornerstone of lasting financial success. Relying on one income source is risky, but multiple streams offer security and growth potential.

Key Takeaways:

- Diversify your income sources to minimize financial risk.
- Leverage earned income to build passive income streams.
- Invest in appreciating assets to ensure long-term growth.
- Automate and scale your income streams to build sustainable wealth.
- Overcome fears and start small—growth follows action.

By mastering the art of creating multiple income streams, you set yourself up for financial security, wealth accumulation, and long-term success. In the next chapter, we'll explore the power of networking and relationships in wealth creation.

CHAPTER 7: THE POWER OF NETWORKING AND RELATIONSHIPS IN WEALTH CREATION

Introduction

Wealthy individuals understand that success is rarely a solitary achievement. They leverage the power of networking and strategic relationships to create opportunities, access exclusive information, and expand their wealth. As Leon Howard famously said, *"Your network determines your net worth."* This chapter explores how the wealthy build and nurture valuable connections that unlock financial success.

In *The Unstoppable Road to Wealth Creation*, I emphasized the importance of the right relationships in opening doors that talent and hard work alone cannot. Networking is not just about meeting people; it's about cultivating meaningful relationships that foster growth and wealth accumulation.

Why Networking is Crucial for Wealth Building

Networking offers several key advantages for wealth creation:

1. **Access to Opportunities** – The right connections introduce you to investments, partnerships, and lucrative deals.
2. **Knowledge and Mentorship** – Learning from those who have already succeeded can help you avoid costly mistakes and fast-track your progress.
3. **Business Growth** – Entrepreneurs and professionals benefit from referrals, collaborations, and funding through their networks.
4. **Social Capital** – Wealth is not just financial. Social capital strengthens influence and creates opportunities.
5. **Leverage and Influence** – The ability to mobilize resources and expertise from a strong network accelerates success.

"The richest people in the world look for and build networks, everyone else looks for work." – Robert Kiyosaki

Scenario: The Power of a Single Connection

Consider Michael, an aspiring entrepreneur who attends an investment seminar and meets a venture capitalist interested in funding start-ups. Through their conversations, the investor introduces him to key industry leaders and funds his business. Within a year, Michael's start-up thrives. This is the power of strategic networking.

How Wealthy People Build Powerful Networks

They Surround Themselves with Like-Minded Individuals

The wealthy are intentional about the people they associate with. As Wall Street Trapper wisely states, *"If you're the smartest person in your circle, you need a new circle."* They seek individuals who challenge them to grow, provide valuable insights, and open doors to new opportunities.

Actionable Steps:

- Attend conferences, mastermind groups, and exclusive networking events.
- Engage in conversations that foster learning and mutual benefit.

They Offer Value Before Seeking Favours

Networking is about building genuine relationships, not simply seeking personal gain. The wealthy understand the law of reciprocity—give first, and you will receive later.

Example:
Sarah, an investor, frequently shares valuable insights on finance forums. Over time, she gains credibility, attracts like-minded professionals, and secures high-profile partnerships.

Actionable Steps:

- Provide mentorship, share knowledge, or introduce valuable contacts without expecting immediate returns.
- Build a reputation for being resourceful and helpful.

They Cultivate Strong Mentorship and Advisory Networks

Mentorship is one of the secret weapons of the wealthy. Robert Greene in *Mastery* states, *"Mentors speed up your learning curve, helping you avoid mistakes and capitalize on opportunities."* Every successful individual has benefited from the guidance of those ahead of them.

Example:
Mark Zuckerberg had Steve Jobs as a mentor. Bill Gates was mentored by Warren Buffett. These relationships significantly shaped their financial decisions and leadership abilities.

Actionable Steps:

- Identify and reach out to mentors in your field.
- Offer assistance or seek guidance, ensuring you respect their time.

They Leverage Exclusive Networks

Elite business clubs, high-net-worth gatherings, and investment circles provide access to lucrative opportunities unavailable to the general public.

Example:
Many billionaires are part of private investment groups where they exchange valuable financial insights and secure deals that the general public can't access.

Actionable Steps:

- Join business and investment clubs.
- Attend elite networking events where top professionals gather.

5. **They Utilize Social Media and Digital Networking**

Platforms such as LinkedIn, Twitter, and industry-specific forums are powerful tools for building relationships globally.

Actionable Steps:

- Engage with industry leaders online by commenting on and sharing their insights.
- Connect with professionals in your field and contribute meaningfully to discussions.

"The richest people in the world are those who have mastered the art of connecting people." – Keith Ferrazzi

Overcoming Networking Challenges

Many people struggle with networking due to fear, shyness, or lack of confidence. However, the wealthy develop strategies to navigate these barriers and turn them into opportunities.

Common Networking Barriers and How to Overcome Them:

1. **Introversion or Social Anxiety?** – Start with online networking and gradually transition to in-person events when you feel more comfortable.
2. **Fear of Rejection?** – Understand that networking is about mutual benefit. Not everyone will respond, but persistence pays off.
3. **Lack of Opportunities?** – Proactively seek out events, forums, and communities where like-minded individuals gather.

"It's not who you know, it's who knows you." – Jeff Bezos

Conclusion: Your Network is Your Greatest Asset

Wealth is rarely built in isolation. Strategic relationships accelerate success, providing access to opportunities, knowledge, and influence.

Key Takeaways:

✅ Surround yourself with people who elevate your mindset and financial success.

✅ Give value first—networking is about mutual benefit, not just taking.

✅ Find mentors and advisors who can guide your wealth-building journey.

✅ Leverage elite business networks and digital platforms to expand opportunities.

✅ Overcome networking fears by practicing engagement and persistence.

Next, in Chapter 8, we will explore how the wealthy invest wisely to multiply their financial success.

CHAPTER 8: INVESTING WISELY – HOW THE WEALTHY MULTIPLY THEIR FINANCIAL SUCCESS

Introduction

Wealthy individuals don't just earn money—they make their money work for them. The ability to invest wisely is one of the most important factors that separates the financially successful from those who struggle. Warren Buffett, one of the most successful investors of all time, famously said, *"The stock market is designed to transfer money from the Active to the Patient."* This quote highlights the power of long-term investment strategies and the discipline necessary to build lasting wealth.

In *The Unstoppable Road to Wealth Creation*, I emphasized that investing is not simply about putting money into assets; it's about understanding risk, making informed decisions, and thinking long-term. In this chapter, we will examine the investment strategies that wealthy individuals use to multiply their wealth and secure their financial futures.

Why the Wealthy Prioritize Investing

Wealthy individuals view investing as an essential part of their financial strategy. Here's why:

1. **Money Grows Over Time** – Through compound interest and capital appreciation, investments generate wealth without requiring constant labour.
2. **Financial Freedom** – Investments create passive income, reducing dependence on active work.
3. **Protection Against Inflation** – Smart investments help preserve and increase purchasing power over time.
4. **Generational Wealth** – Wise investments ensure long-term financial security for future generations.
5. **Leverage and Expansion** – Wealthy individuals use investments to grow businesses, acquire assets, and build more wealth.

"Do not save what is left after spending, but spend what is left after saving." – Warren Buffett

Scenario: The Power of Early Investment

Imagine two friends, John and Peter. John begins investing $500 a month at age 25, while Peter waits until he's 40 to start investing the same amount. Even though they both invest the same sum, John's wealth grows nearly twice as large as Peter's by the time they both retire—thanks to the power of compounding. This example illustrates the importance of starting early and investing consistently.

Investment Strategies of the Wealthy

They Invest in Assets, Not Liabilities

Robert Kiyosaki, author of *Rich Dad Poor Dad*, famously said, *"The rich buy assets. The poor only have expenses. The middle class buys liabilities they think are assets."* Wealthy individuals focus on acquiring assets that generate income or appreciate in value, such as:

- **Stocks** – Ownership in companies that provide dividends and capital gains.
- **Real Estate** – Rental properties, land, and commercial buildings.
- **Businesses** – Investing in or acquiring profitable ventures.
- **Intellectual Property** – Books, patents, and digital content that generate royalties.

Actionable Step:

- Conduct an asset-liability assessment to ensure that your purchases are generating wealth, not draining it.
- Prioritize acquiring assets that increase in value or produce passive income.

They Diversify Their Investments

Leon Howard states, *"Never put all your eggs in one basket unless you are prepared to watch that basket very closely."* The wealthy understand that diversification reduces risk while maximizing potential returns.

Example:
Sarah, a successful investor, divides her wealth into stocks, real estate, bonds, and alternative investments like cryptocurrency. When the stock market dips, her other investments help maintain financial stability.

Actionable Step:

- Balance your portfolio across various asset classes.
- Invest in both low-risk and high-return opportunities.

They Leverage the Power of Compounding

Albert Einstein famously called compound interest *"the eighth wonder of the world."* The wealthy invest early and reinvest earnings to grow their wealth over time.

Example:
If you invest $10,000 in an asset with an 8% annual return, in 30 years, your investment could grow to over $100,000, thanks to the magic of compounding.

Actionable Step:

- Start investing early and reinvest profits.
- Choose long-term investment vehicles, such as index funds and dividend stocks, that benefit from compounding.

They Invest in Themselves First

Robert Greene, in *The 48 Laws of Power*, emphasizes that *"The investment in yourself is the most important investment you will ever make."* Wealthy individuals prioritize personal growth, education, and skill-building, which empowers them to make smarter investment choices.

Actionable Step:

- Take courses on finance, investing, and wealth-building.
- Read books and follow mentors in your areas of interest.

They Take Calculated Risks

The wealthy embrace risk, but they do so with careful planning and research. Instead of gambling, they assess potential outcomes before taking the plunge.

Example:
Elon Musk invested nearly all of his PayPal earnings into Tesla and SpaceX, risking financial ruin. His calculated risks ultimately turned him into one of the world's wealthiest individuals.

Actionable Step:

- Evaluate the risk-reward ratios before making any investment decision.
- Consult with experts and conduct in-depth research before diving into unfamiliar investments.

They Use Other People's Money (OPM) Wisely

Wealthy investors understand how to use debt and financing to grow their investments. They use *good debt*—debt that is used to acquire income-generating assets, rather than *bad debt*—debt used for consumer spending that drains wealth.

Example:
David secures a loan to purchase a rental property. His tenants' rent covers the mortgage, while he profits from both rental income and the appreciation of the property.

Actionable Step:

- Learn the difference between good debt (for investment) and bad debt (for consumption).
- Use borrowed funds only for assets that generate income.

Overcoming Investment Challenges

Many people hesitate to invest due to fear, lack of knowledge, or limited capital. However, the wealthy overcome these obstacles with strategic planning and action.

Common Investment Challenges and How to Overcome Them:

1. **Not Enough Money?** – Start small with index funds, fractional shares, or automated investing platforms.
2. **Fear of Losing Money?** – Educate yourself, and focus on low-risk, long-term assets.
3. **Lack of Knowledge?** – Read financial books, follow investment experts, and take online courses to build expertise.

"The goal is not to make money, but to create wealth." – Tony Robbins

Conclusion: Invest Like the Wealthy

Wealth is not just about earning—it's about investing wisely, allowing your money to grow over time. The wealthy achieve financial independence by strategically allocating resources, managing risks, and leveraging financial tools to build more wealth.

Key Takeaways:

✅ Buy assets that appreciate in value and generate passive income.

✅ Diversify investments to minimize risk.

✅ Start investing early and take advantage of compounding.

✅ Invest in yourself to increase your financial literacy.

✅ Take calculated risks and use leverage wisely.

By applying these principles, you will be well on your way to building financial growth and long-term prosperity. In the next chapter, we will explore how the wealthy master financial discipline and avoid the traps of overspending.

CHAPTER 9: FINANCIAL DISCIPLINE – THE WEALTHY MASTER THEIR MONEY, NOT THE OTHER WAY AROUND

Introduction

Financial discipline is the bedrock of wealth creation. Wealthy individuals do not only focus on earning and investing wisely, but they also excel in managing their expenses, controlling cash flow, and making prudent financial decisions. As Warren Buffett wisely said, "Do not save what is left after spending, but spend what is left after saving." This chapter delves into how wealthy individuals maintain stringent financial discipline, sidestepping the common financial pitfalls that prevent many from achieving lasting prosperity.

In *The Unstoppable Road to Wealth Creation*, I emphasized that financial discipline isn't about deprivation; it's about understanding your priorities and ensuring every dollar serves a meaningful purpose. Let's explore the strategies that help the wealthy stay financially disciplined and build long-term wealth.

Why Financial Discipline is Crucial for Wealth Building

1. **Preserves Wealth Across Generations** – Without discipline, even enormous fortunes can be lost over time.
2. **Prevents Lifestyle Inflation** – As income increases, wealthy individuals resist the temptation to increase their spending.
3. **Ensures Long-Term Security** – Wise management of money helps protect against financial uncertainties.
4. **Opens Investment Opportunities** – Maintaining financial discipline allows the wealthy to seize favourable opportunities when they arise.
5. **Mitigates Debt and Reduces Financial Stress** – The wealthy understand the importance of managing debt and avoid unnecessary financial burdens.

Scenario: The Lottery Winner vs. The Disciplined Investor

James wins $10 million in the lottery but squanders it through careless spending within five years. Meanwhile, Peter, a disciplined investor, earns the same amount over time and makes careful financial decisions, ensuring his wealth continues to grow. This comparison highlights that wealth isn't just about acquiring money—it's about retaining and growing it.

Financial Discipline Strategies of the Wealthy

1. They Follow a Strict Budget

The wealthy track their income and expenses diligently. They prioritize essential needs and investments over frivolous indulgences.

Example:

Oprah Winfrey, despite her immense wealth, remains disciplined in her approach to managing money. She stresses the importance of spending with intention, ensuring every dollar contributes to her long-term financial goals.

Actionable Step:

• Create a monthly budget with fixed allocations for savings, investments, and necessary expenses.

• Use apps or tools to track your spending habits and identify areas to cut back.

2. They Pay Themselves First

Wealthy individuals prioritize saving and investing before spending. This approach ensures that wealth creation remains the main focus.

Quote from Warren Buffett:

"If you buy things you do not need, soon you will have to sell things you need."

Actionable Step:

• Automate your savings by directing a percentage of your income into investment accounts before spending on discretionary items.

3. They Avoid Impulse Spending and Emotional Purchases

The wealthy avoid the trap of emotional spending—making unnecessary purchases driven by stress, excitement, or peer pressure. Instead, they make thoughtful financial decisions.

Example:

Jeff Bezos, despite his immense fortune, is known for his frugal and minimalist approach to spending. His focus remains on long-term growth rather than short-term gratification.

Actionable Step:

• Implement the 48-hour rule—wait 48 hours before making any non-essential purchases.

• Differentiate between needs and wants to ensure intentional spending.

4. **They Avoid Bad Debt and Leverage Good Debt Wisely**

The wealthy understand that not all debt is bad. They distinguish between "good" debt, used for investments, real estate, or business growth, and "bad" debt, used for non-productive consumption.

Example:

Elon Musk effectively uses debt to finance the growth of Tesla, ensuring that it yields substantial returns in the future.

Actionable Step:

- Avoid high-interest debt, such as credit card balances.
- Use loans strategically to invest in income-generating assets.

5. **They Live Below Their Means—Even When Rich**

Wealthy individuals often do not flaunt their wealth. Instead, they focus on long-term financial security and wealth accumulation, not on appearances.

Quote from Wall Street Trapper:

"Don't flex to impress—invest to progress."

Example:

Mark Zuckerberg, despite being a billionaire, drives a modest car. His priority is wealth growth and investment, not social validation.

Actionable Step:

- Resist the urge to upgrade your lifestyle when income increases.
- Focus on building lasting wealth rather than displaying temporary affluence.

6. **They Have Emergency Funds and Financial Safety Nets**

The wealthy are prepared for financial downturns by maintaining cash reserves and emergency funds.

Example:

During the 2008 financial crisis, individuals with strong financial discipline used their savings to purchase undervalued assets, which later appreciated significantly.

Actionable Step:

- Maintain an emergency fund with at least 6 months' worth of living expenses.

• Invest in liquid assets that can be accessed in times of need.

7. **They Continuously Educate Themselves on Financial Management**

Financial literacy is an ongoing process for the wealthy. They regularly read books, attend seminars, and seek mentorship to enhance their financial knowledge and discipline.

Quote from Robert Greene:

"The future belongs to those who learn more skills and combine them in creative ways."

Actionable Step:

• Read books on finance and wealth-building, such as *The Unstoppable Road to Wealth Creation.*

• Follow experts and attend workshops to stay updated on financial strategies.

Overcoming Financial Discipline Challenges

Many struggle with maintaining financial discipline due to poor habits, social pressures, or lack of financial knowledge. However, anyone can develop better money management skills with conscious effort and perseverance.

Common Challenges and How to Overcome Them:

1. **Struggling with Budgeting?** – Start with simple methods and gradually refine your budgeting practices.
2. **Tempted to Overspend?** – Implement a waiting period before making large purchases, especially non-essential ones.
3. **Drowning in Debt?** – Focus on paying off high-interest loans first while building your emergency fund.

Conclusion: Mastering Financial Discipline for Long-Term Wealth

True financial success is not solely about earning money—it's about managing it effectively. Wealthy individuals maintain financial discipline by creating and sticking to budgets, saving aggressively, avoiding bad debt, and continuing to learn.

Key Takeaways:

✅ Track income and expenses with a strict budget.

✅ Pay yourself first—save and invest before spending.

✅ Resist impulse spending and prioritize needs over wants.

✅ Use debt wisely and focus on wealth-building opportunities.

✅ Live below your means, even as your income grows.

✅ Keep an emergency fund for financial protection.

✅ Continuously invest in financial education and skill-building.

By applying these principles of financial discipline, you set yourself up for long-lasting wealth and financial freedom. In the next chapter, we will delve into how the wealthy use strategic philanthropy and giving to not only benefit others but also further enhance their financial legacy.

CHAPTER 10: THE POWER OF LEVERAGE AND NETWORKING – USING OTHER PEOPLE'S MONEY, TIME, AND SKILLS

Introduction

The key to financial success is not just about working harder—it's about working smarter. True wealth creation is often fuelled by leverage—the ability to multiply resources using other people's money (OPM), time (OPT), skills (OPS), and influence (OPI). This chapter will delve into how leveraging these resources is a game changer for wealth accumulation and how you can apply this principle effectively to accelerate your financial growth.

As Robert Kiyosaki, author of *Rich Dad Poor Dad*, wisely puts it, "The rich don't work for money; they make money work for them." This mindset is at the core of how the wealthy scale their wealth beyond their own efforts. By mastering the art of leverage, they create wealth far more efficiently than those who only rely on their personal resources.

Understanding Leverage in Wealth Building

Leverage, in financial terms, is the use of external resources to enhance returns on investment. This concept can be applied in various ways, from financial capital to human and social capital. Let's break it down into four key types of leverage:

1. **Financial Leverage** – Using borrowed capital to amplify returns on investments.
2. **Time Leverage** – Delegating tasks to free up your personal time for higher-value activities.
3. **Skill Leverage** – Employing experts to handle tasks that are beyond your own expertise.
4. **Network Leverage** – Harnessing relationships to access opportunities that wouldn't otherwise be available.

Scenario: The Self-Made Millionaire vs. The Leveraged Millionaire

John, a self-employed consultant, works 80 hours a week and earns £200,000 annually. He's limited by the amount of time he can dedicate to his work.

Michael, on the other hand, is an entrepreneur who uses a combination of external funding and skilled team members. He makes £1 million annually—without working nearly as many hours.

What's the difference? Leverage. As Michael's success shows, wealth doesn't always come from working harder but from using available resources effectively.

1. Financial Leverage: Using Other People's Money (OPM)

Wealthy individuals and businesses don't rely solely on their own funds to finance their ventures. Instead, they use other people's money—such as loans or investments—to fuel their growth.

Examples of Financial Leverage:

- **Real Estate Investing:** Investors often use mortgages to purchase properties, allowing them to control large assets with minimal personal capital.
- **Stock Market:** Investors use margin trading to borrow funds from brokers and amplify their purchasing power.
- **Business Expansion:** Entrepreneurs take out loans or attract investors to scale their businesses much faster.

As Wall Street Trapper states, "The wealthy don't save money—they move money." The rich don't hoard cash; they put it to work, allowing them to create more wealth over time.

Actionable Step:

Instead of focusing solely on saving, direct your money into assets that generate passive income.

2. Time Leverage: Using Other People's Time (OPT)

Time is the one resource that cannot be replenished. The wealthy know how to make the most of their time by outsourcing, automating, and focusing on high-value tasks only.

Examples of Time Leverage:

- Hiring employees or virtual assistants to handle routine tasks.
- Automating processes like accounting, customer service, and marketing.

- Investing in passive income streams to generate money without daily effort.

As Leon Howard puts it, "Rich people buy time; poor people sell time." The wealthy use others' time to maximize their own output.

Actionable Step:

Identify areas of your life or business where you can outsource or automate tasks, freeing up your time for more strategic activities.

3. Skill Leverage: Using Other People's Skills (OPS)

The wealthy understand they cannot do everything themselves. Instead, they hire specialists who bring expertise in areas outside their knowledge.

Examples of Skill Leverage:

- Hiring professionals such as accountants, legal advisors, or financial planners.
- Collaborating with specialists like marketers, designers, or business consultants.
- Building a team to efficiently execute business tasks.

As Robert Greene, author of *The 48 Laws of Power*, wisely notes: "Never do yourself what others can do for you." Successful people focus on what they do best and delegate the rest.

Actionable Step:

Recognize tasks that are outside your skill set and delegate them to experts who can execute them better and faster.

4. Network Leverage: Using Other People's Influence (OPI)

Surrounding yourself with the right people is critical to wealth building. Wealthy individuals leverage their networks to access opportunities, resources, and knowledge that are otherwise out of reach.

Examples of Network Leverage:

- Joining mastermind groups to learn from others' experiences and insights.
- Partnering with influencers to expand your reach and grow your brand.
- Building strategic alliances to open doors to new business opportunities.

Warren Buffett, one of the wealthiest individuals in the world, says, "The best investment you can make is in your network." Building and nurturing relationships with the right people can propel you toward success faster than almost any other strategy.

Actionable Step:

Attend networking events, join professional organizations, and build relationships with individuals who can provide access to valuable resources.

Overcoming the Fear of Leverage

Despite its potential, many people are afraid to use leverage due to the perceived risks involved—fear of debt, loss, or losing control. However, when used wisely, leverage can be a powerful tool for creating wealth.

How to Use Leverage Wisely:

1. **Understand the Risks** – Leverage can amplify losses as much as it can amplify gains.
2. **Start Small** – Begin with manageable amounts of leverage, such as low-interest loans or small investments.
3. **Seek Expert Advice** – Always consult with financial advisors or experts before making large leveraged decisions.
4. **Monitor and Adjust** – Regularly evaluate the performance of your leveraged investments to ensure they remain profitable.

Conclusion: Mastering Leverage for Wealth Creation

Leverage isn't about taking shortcuts; it's about using available resources strategically to multiply your wealth. The rich know how to use other people's money, time, skills, and influence to unlock opportunities and create exponential growth.

Key Takeaways:

✅ Use Other People's Money (OPM) to invest in assets that generate income.

✅ Leverage Other People's Time (OPT) to free up your time for higher-value activities.

✅ Delegate tasks to Other People's Skills (OPS) for greater efficiency.

✅ Build relationships and expand opportunities through Other People's Influence (OPI).

✅ Learn to manage and assess the risks of leverage to maximize its potential.

By mastering the art of leverage, you can achieve financial independence faster and scale your wealth beyond what you thought possible. In the next chapter, we'll dive into investing for long-term wealth—an essential step in preserving and growing your financial success.

PART 3:

BUSINESS AND ENTREPRENEURSHIP

CHAPTER 11: THINKING LIKE A BUSINESS OWNER – WHY THE WEALTHY DON'T TRADE TIME FOR MONEY

Introduction

The journey to wealth involves strategic shifts in how one views money and time. In *The Unstoppable Road to Wealth Creation*, I emphasized the importance of moving beyond a "job mindset" to a "wealth-building mindset." This transition is central to understanding why the wealthy don't trade their time for money. They focus on building systems, businesses, and investments that continue generating wealth without requiring constant effort.

In *The Things Wealthy People Do*, we explore how the wealthy take ownership of their financial destiny. While most people work hard for a paycheck, the wealthy work smart by creating income streams that run on autopilot, allowing them to achieve financial independence.

Employee vs. Business Owner Mindset

In *The Unstoppable Road to Wealth Creation*, I highlight how the wealthy differentiate themselves by adopting an entrepreneurial mindset. As I pointed out in Chapter 3, "A business is an engine that runs even when you're not there." This sentiment mirrors the philosophy of *The Things Wealthy People Do*. While employees trade time for money, business owners leverage systems to generate revenue with minimal personal involvement.

Example:

- **Employee Mindset:** Someone working 9-5 might make a salary of £40,000 per year, but their financial growth is limited by their time and effort.
- **Business Owner Mindset:** The wealthy business owner, by contrast, may scale a product, system, or service, and generate revenue even while on vacation or at home. This is the core principle of not trading time for money, which we emphasize in both books.

Why the Wealthy Don't Trade Time for Money

A recurring theme in both *The Unstoppable Road to Wealth Creation* and *The Things Wealthy People Do* is that the wealthy understand time is their most valuable resource. In Chapter 5 of *The Unstoppable Road to Wealth Creation*, I discuss "Time as Currency," where I stress that true wealth comes from managing time efficiently by leveraging others' skills and time. The wealthy build systems and processes that allow their businesses to run efficiently without constant supervision.

As stated in this book, *The Things Wealthy People Do*, "True wealth comes from ownership and systems that generate income autonomously." This connects perfectly with the teachings in *The Unstoppable Road to Wealth Creation*, where I emphasize that you can build financial freedom through scalable, passive income streams.

Business Ownership: Creating Scalable Income

In *The Unstoppable Road to Wealth Creation*, one of the key lessons is that wealth is built by creating assets, not just earning wages. This is exactly what is detailed in this book, *The Things Wealthy People Do*. While many people focus on earning money by trading hours, the wealthy know that building a business or an investment that creates wealth is the key to long-term success.

Example from The Unstoppable Road to Wealth Creation:

I use the example of real estate investments to illustrate how assets can generate income. Similarly, in *The Things Wealthy People Do*, we see that wealthy individuals invest in assets such as stocks, real estate, or businesses that can earn them money over time. This is not just about making money now but positioning oneself for future wealth.

Actionable Step from The Unstoppable Road to Wealth Creation:

Consider the principle of "asset accumulation" I discuss in Chapter 8 of my book. Whether it's through real estate, stocks, or even a successful business, accumulate assets that can generate income passively. This aligns directly with the business ownership strategies in *The Things Wealthy People Do*, where passive income is emphasized as a crucial element of wealth-building.

Creating Systems: Earning While You Sleep

The Unstoppable Road to Wealth Creation highlights how important it is to build businesses that work for you. By establishing automated systems, leveraging technology, and outsourcing tasks, the wealthy create income streams that don't require their direct, constant involvement.

Example:

In Chapter 7 of *The Unstoppable Road to Wealth Creation*, I explain how online business models like e-commerce or digital products enable creators to earn money while they sleep. This concept aligns directly with this book, *The Things Wealthy People Do*, where we delve into how creating scalable businesses and systems frees the business owner from trading hours for money.

Actionable Step from The Unstoppable Road to Wealth Creation:

Build your business on a foundation that allows for automation, like creating a membership-based service or using digital products to generate income without requiring constant time investment. This is the core principle of both books, emphasizing that automation and systems create a path to true financial freedom.

Leveraging Other People's Resources (OPR): Using People to Build Your Business

In *The Unstoppable Road to Wealth Creation*, I discuss the importance of delegating and outsourcing tasks to create a leverageable business. This book, *The Things Wealthy People Do* reiterates this idea by focusing on the power of leveraging other people's time, skills, and resources to scale quickly.

Example:

In my book, I mention how successful entrepreneurs understand the value of hiring skilled professionals to handle areas where they lack expertise—whether it's finance, marketing, or operations. This same concept is explored in *The Things Wealthy People Do*, where wealth-building is attributed to the ability to collaborate and delegate effectively.

Actionable Step from The Unstoppable Road to Wealth Creation:

If you're running a business, consider areas you can delegate to experts. Whether it's hiring an accountant or a marketing team, leveraging others' expertise allows you to focus on growing the business. This principle is reinforced in *The Things Wealthy People Do*, where delegating non-core tasks to experts allows the business owner to focus on high-impact work.

Conclusion: Thinking Like a Business Owner

In both *The Unstoppable Road to Wealth Creation* and *The Things Wealthy People Do*, the central idea is clear: the wealthy don't trade time for money. They build systems, own businesses, and create assets that generate wealth passively. As I discussed in *The Unstoppable Road to Wealth Creation*, wealth-building requires adopting a mindset that values ownership, strategic planning, and leveraging other people's resources. By thinking like a business owner, you can transcend the limits of time and achieve financial independence.

Key Takeaways:

- **Adopt an Entrepreneurial Mindset:** Like in *The Unstoppable Road to Wealth Creation*, understand the importance of creating scalable businesses that generate income beyond your direct involvement.
- **Create Systems and Automate:** Systems, as detailed in both books, allow you to earn money without constantly working.

- **Leverage Other People's Resources:** In *The Unstoppable Road to Wealth Creation*, I emphasize that collaboration and delegation are key to expanding your wealth.

By combining the insights from both books, you can accelerate your journey toward financial freedom and build wealth that isn't tied to trading time for money.

CHAPTER 12: CREATING GENERATIONAL WEALTH – BUILDING A LEGACY THAT LASTS

Introduction

True wealth is not defined by how much money you accumulate, but by what you leave behind for future generations. This concept has been embraced by some of the wealthiest families in history—from the Rockefellers to the Rothschilds. These families understood that generational wealth isn't just about money; it's about creating lasting opportunities, financial security, and knowledge for the future.

As I emphasized in *The Unstoppable Road to Wealth Creation*, wealth-building is not simply about working hard for the present, but setting up systems that work for you across multiple generations. Warren Buffett famously said, *"Someone is sitting in the shade today because someone planted a tree a long time ago."* The question for us is: are we planting those trees today?

This chapter will delve into the principles of generational wealth—how the wealthy pass down their knowledge, strategies, and financial security—and how you can do the same to ensure your wealth benefits future generations.

The Importance of Generational Wealth

Generational wealth is about more than just money. It's about building a foundation that ensures your descendants are financially secure, educated, and able to capitalize on opportunities that you may never have had access to. This wealth-building mindset connects directly with the ideas I discussed in *The Unstoppable Road to Wealth Creation*. Just as I emphasize in my book that *true wealth lies in the ability to create assets, not just accumulate cash*, generational wealth extends this idea to include not only financial assets but also knowledge and opportunities that can shape future generations.

Here's why generational wealth matters:

1. **Financial Security** – By investing wisely and creating lasting systems, you ensure your family won't face financial hardship, just as I outlined in Chapter 5 of *The Unstoppable Road to Wealth Creation*, where I emphasized the importance of building passive income streams that don't require constant work.
2. **Access to Better Opportunities** – With wealth comes the ability to open doors for future generations. Whether it's better educational opportunities or access to capital to invest in businesses, wealth ensures that your children and their children have more than you did.
3. **Economic Power & Influence** – Wealthy families shape industries, policies, and global economies. As seen in *The Unstoppable Road to Wealth Creation*, ownership gives you influence, and the more assets you control, the greater your ability to impact the world.

4. **A Lasting Legacy** – As I mention in my book, *You cannot build wealth if it's lost after one generation.* Building generational wealth is about ensuring that the money and opportunities you create continue to benefit your family for decades.
5. **Freedom & Choices** – Generational wealth provides the luxury of choice. It frees future generations to pursue their passions without being held back by financial constraints.

Scenario: The Wealth-Builder vs. The Consumer

Consider two individuals:

- **David**, a self-made millionaire, invests in assets such as real estate, businesses, and stocks. He teaches his children about the importance of financial literacy and how to manage and grow wealth.
- **Paul**, a high-income earner, spends everything he makes on a lavish lifestyle and leaves nothing for his family to inherit.

In fifty years, David's descendants inherit his wealth, education, and business empire, continuing to grow it. Paul's family, however, struggles financially because there is no system in place for sustaining wealth. The key difference here is the wealth-building mindset—a principle I outline in Chapter 2 of *The Unstoppable Road to Wealth Creation.*

Principles of Generational Wealth Creation

To build lasting wealth, the wealthy follow specific principles. These principles ensure that wealth is protected and passed down for generations, and they align with the core lessons from *The Unstoppable Road to Wealth Creation.*

1. Ownership Mentality – Control Assets, Not Just Money

The wealthy understand the value of owning assets that appreciate over time. It's not enough to just earn money; you must put that money into investments that will continue to generate wealth long after you're gone.

- **Real Estate:** Properties that generate rental income and appreciate in value over time.
- **Businesses:** Ownership in companies, particularly family-owned businesses, provides long-term cash flow and the potential for growth.
- **Stocks & Investments:** Holding shares in major corporations helps ensure your wealth grows, even during economic downturns.
- **Intellectual Property:** Patents, trademarks, and royalties from books or inventions can continue to generate revenue for generations.

As I pointed out in *The Unstoppable Road to Wealth Creation*, wealth-building isn't just about increasing your earnings but rather about securing income-generating assets that allow you to pass down long-term security.

2. Financial Education – Teach the Next Generation

One of the key reasons families lose wealth over generations is the lack of financial education. In *The Unstoppable Road to Wealth Creation*, I discuss how families should be intentional about teaching financial literacy and the importance of making informed investment decisions.

- Educate your children on money management, investing, and building businesses.
- Encourage them to seek out mentors, read financial books, and attend seminars.

- Help them develop the habit of avoiding debt and building diverse income streams.

3. Estate Planning & Wealth Protection

Ensuring your wealth is properly protected and passed down is vital to avoiding future disputes and ensuring financial security for the next generation. This is why estate planning is a crucial part of generational wealth, as I emphasize in Chapter 7 of *The Unstoppable Road to Wealth Creation.*

- **Trust Funds:** Protect assets from taxation and mismanagement.
- **Wills & Estate Plans:** Prevent wealth from being lost in legal battles and ensure a smooth transfer of assets.
- **Life Insurance:** Provides an additional layer of protection and ensures your descendants have financial stability.

Quote from Robert Kiyosaki:
"It's not about how much money you make, but how much you keep, how hard it works for you, and how many generations you keep it for."

Wealth Strategies the Rich Use

Many of the world's wealthiest families have built generational wealth by adopting specific strategies that preserve and grow their fortune. These methods are echoed in the principles I highlight in *The Unstoppable Road to Wealth Creation.*

1. The Rockefeller Method: Family Trusts

The Rockefeller family used trusts to create multi-generational wealth, ensuring that their assets were protected from taxation and mismanagement. Family members receive structured distributions, ensuring the wealth remains intact for future generations.

2. Investing in Real Estate & Land

Real estate has been a cornerstone of wealth for centuries. Whether through rental properties, commercial real estate, or agricultural land, owning land ensures long-term financial stability. This concept ties directly into the wealth-building strategies I describe in *The Unstoppable Road to Wealth Creation*, where I explain that real estate offers both income and appreciation.

3. Creating Family Businesses

Family businesses provide ongoing wealth and legacy, as seen with families like the Waltons (Walmart) and the Rothschilds. As I outline in *The Unstoppable Road to Wealth Creation*, starting a family business allows wealth to be built and passed down without the reliance on external employers or markets.

4. Using Life Insurance for Wealth Building

Many wealthy families use life insurance to create a tax-free inheritance, and strategies like the Infinite Banking Concept (IBC) allow individuals to build a private family bank. I discuss the importance of using insurance policies as a financial tool in *The Unstoppable Road to Wealth Creation*, where I highlight them as an essential component of a well-rounded wealth plan.

Avoiding the Pitfalls of Wealth Erosion

Even the wealthiest families can lose everything if they mismanage their wealth. This concept ties into what I discuss in *The Unstoppable Road to Wealth Creation*, where I explain that without a proper financial education and wealth protection plan, families risk losing everything.

Common Mistakes That Destroy Generational Wealth:

Lack of Financial Education

Overspending & Lifestyle Inflation

Poor Investments & Business Decisions

High Taxes & Poor Estate Planning

Family Conflicts Over Inheritance

Solution:

- Hold regular family meetings to discuss wealth goals and responsibilities.
- Provide financial literacy programs for younger generations.
- Appoint trusted advisors to manage and protect family wealth.

Quote from Robert Greene:
"Power is fleeting unless you establish systems that sustain it."

Steps to Start Building Generational Wealth Today

1. Invest in appreciating assets like real estate, stocks, and businesses.
2. Set up a family trust to protect and pass on wealth.
3. Educate your children on financial management and investment strategies.
4. Create a solid estate plan, including wills and life insurance.
5. Foster an entrepreneurial mindset within the family.
6. Build relationships with other wealthy individuals and mentors.
7. Think long-term—your wealth isn't for today, but for future generations.

Conclusion: The Legacy You Leave Behind

Building generational wealth requires long-term vision, commitment, and the right strategies. The wealthy don't just focus on accumulating wealth for themselves—they focus on creating systems that will ensure their family's prosperity for generations to come. As I emphasize in *The Unstoppable Road to Wealth Creation*, wealth-building is a lifelong journey that requires careful planning and consistent action.

By applying the principles discussed in both books, you can create a lasting legacy that benefits your family for years to come. The future of your descendants starts with the decisions you make today.

Key Takeaways:

- Wealth is preserved through ownership, education, and proper planning.
- Real estate, businesses, and investments create long-term financial security.
- Trusts, wills, and life insurance protect and transfer wealth efficiently.
- Financial literacy ensures wealth doesn't disappear.
- Legacy-building is a long-term strategy, not a quick fix.

In the next chapter, we'll explore how the wealthy scale, expand and grow their businesses.

CHAPTER 13: SCALING AND EXPANDING – HOW THE RICH GROW THEIR BUSINESSES

Introduction

Wealth is not solely about accumulating assets; it's about creating systems that can grow and multiply. Scaling and expanding your business are essential strategies for building long-term wealth. In *The Unstoppable Road to Wealth Creation*, I emphasize that successful business owners focus on building scalable systems, not just businesses. This chapter delves into the key strategies that wealthy individuals use to expand their businesses, ensuring sustained success and growth. Scaling your business allows you to move from simply being a business owner to becoming a true wealth creator.

Why Scaling Your Business Matters

The wealthy understand the difference between owning a business that sustains them and building one that can operate and thrive without their constant involvement. As I discussed in *The Unstoppable Road to Wealth Creation*, scaling allows you to **amplify** your efforts, assets, and resources. It's not just about managing a business; it's about building one that can grow beyond your active participation.

Here's why scaling is crucial:

1. **Increased Revenue** – Scaling lets your business grow without a proportional rise in costs, leading to exponential profit growth.
2. **Market Leadership** – As your business expands, you can dominate your industry by reaching more customers and offering more value.
3. **Sustainability** – A scalable business is built for the long haul, ensuring its success even without direct involvement.
4. **Wealth Creation** – Scaling your business creates ongoing wealth by building systems that generate income over time. This aligns with the principles outlined in *The Unstoppable Road to Wealth Creation*, where creating passive income is key.

How the Wealthy Scale Their Businesses

Scaling requires deliberate strategy and consistent effort. It's not about working harder but about working smarter and leveraging the right opportunities.

1. Building Robust Systems and Processes

The wealthy know that in order to scale effectively, their business needs strong systems and processes that can operate smoothly without direct intervention. This includes automating tasks, delegating work, and streamlining operations.

- **Automation:** Technology helps automate repetitive tasks, making operations more efficient and freeing up time.
- **Outsourcing:** Wealthy entrepreneurs understand they can't do everything themselves. By outsourcing tasks, they focus on high-level decisions that drive growth.

In *The Unstoppable Road to Wealth Creation*, I highlight that scaling isn't about doing more work but about creating systems that handle growth without requiring more time from you.

2. Expanding Market Reach

Once you have solid systems in place, the next step is expanding your reach. This can be achieved by entering new markets, diversifying product offerings, and increasing visibility.

- **Geographic Expansion:** Tapping into new cities, countries, or regions increases your customer base and revenue potential.
- **Product Diversification:** Offering new products or services creates new revenue streams and accelerates growth.
- **Digital Strategies:** In today's world, leveraging digital platforms for marketing, sales, and e-commerce is essential to global expansion.

Scaling your business requires recognizing opportunities to reach a larger audience and deliver more value, as discussed in *The Unstoppable Road to Wealth Creation.*

3. Using Other People's Money (OPM)

Wealthy business owners often use leverage to scale. This means using external capital to fund growth while preserving their own capital.

- **Investor Funding:** Raising capital from investors, venture capital, or crowdfunding allows for quicker scaling without relying on personal savings or loans.
- **Strategic Partnerships:** Partnering with other businesses enables resource sharing, extending your reach and accelerating growth.

As I mention in *The Unstoppable Road to Wealth Creation*, leveraging OPM is a powerful way to scale without exposing yourself to excessive financial risk.

4. Building a Strong Team

As your business expands, so does the need for a competent team. Wealthy individuals focus on building strong leadership teams that can manage growth.

- **Hiring for Growth**: Successful entrepreneurs hire experts in different areas such as marketing, operations, and finance, so they can focus on scaling.
- **Leadership Development**: Creating leaders within your organization ensures the business can thrive independently of your direct involvement.

Delegation is key to scaling, as I explain in *The Unstoppable Road to Wealth Creation.* The more you delegate, the more your business can grow without your constant attention.

Challenges of Scaling a Business

Scaling comes with its challenges, even for the wealthiest. It's essential to have a plan to manage these hurdles strategically.

Common challenges include:

- **Cash Flow Issues:** Rapid growth requires significant investment, which can put a strain on cash flow.
- **Operational Strain:** As your business grows, your operations become more complex, requiring new systems.
- **Cultural Shifts:** Maintaining company culture during rapid growth can be difficult.

As I discussed in *The Unstoppable Road to Wealth Creation*, overcoming these challenges requires proper financial planning, strong operational systems, and a focus on maintaining the core values that made your business successful.

Steps to Scale Your Business

If you're looking to scale, consider these steps:

1. **Develop Scalable Systems:** Identify areas for automation and delegate tasks to create efficiency.
2. **Expand Your Market:** Explore new markets and diversify your products to increase your customer base.
3. **Leverage Capital:** Use external funding or strategic partnerships to fuel your growth.
4. **Build a Talented Team:** Hire and develop leaders who can take on the responsibility of managing growth.
5. **Invest in Technology:** Use digital tools to enhance your operations and increase your reach.

6. **Monitor Cash Flow:** Ensure you have the capital to sustain growth without jeopardizing financial stability.

Conclusion: The Power of Scaling

Scaling is an essential part of building wealth. The wealthy understand that it's not about working harder but about creating systems that allow the business to grow and generate wealth long-term. In *The Unstoppable Road to Wealth Creation*, I emphasized the importance of building systems that work for you, and scaling is the process of expanding those systems to maximize your impact and success.

By applying the strategies discussed in this chapter, you'll not only grow your business but also create a platform for lasting wealth. In the next chapter, we'll explore the essence of branding and influence. A strategy used by the wealthy to create lasting value.

CHAPTER 14: THE SIGNIFICANCE OF BRANDING AND INFLUENCE – CREATING ENDURING VALUE

Introduction

In the journey of wealth creation, branding and influence are pivotal. Whether you are developing a personal brand or expanding a business, how the world perceives your products and services is a major determinant of success. As highlighted in *The Unstoppable Road to Wealth Creation*, positioning yourself and your business strategically is key to fostering long-term value. Branding goes beyond logos and slogans—it is about creating a reputation that deeply resonates with your audience, fostering loyalty, and ensuring sustained profits.

This chapter delves into the vital role of branding and influence in wealth creation, the steps to build a timeless brand, and how influence can propel your business forward.

Why Branding and Influence Matter

Branding and influence are integral to business prosperity, especially when it comes to building wealth. Here's why they are crucial:

1. **Building Customer Loyalty** – A strong brand fosters trust, leading to repeat purchases and word-of-mouth referrals.
2. **Standing Out in the Market** – A well-crafted brand differentiates you from competitors and gives you an edge in the market.
3. **Premium Pricing Power** – Strong brands often have the ability to charge higher prices due to the perceived value they offer.
4. **Sustaining Long-Term Value** – Powerful brands build enduring relationships with their audience and are more likely to withstand economic challenges.

As emphasized in *The Unstoppable Road to Wealth Creation*, a strong brand influences wealth creation. When customers believe in your brand, they're not just buying products—they're investing in your mission, values, and legacy.

Building a Strong Brand

Building a successful brand is rooted in authenticity, consistency, and providing value. In *The Unstoppable Road to Wealth Creation*, I discuss how creating a business with a clear vision and purpose, along with a consistent message, can create lasting resonance with your audience. Let's break down the key elements involved in building a strong brand:

1. Clarifying Your Brand's Purpose and Values

A brand without purpose is just a name. The most successful individuals know that a brand needs a clear mission and values that connect with the desires and needs of the target market.

- **Brand Purpose**: What is your brand's mission? What impact do you want to make on your customers and the world?
- **Core Values**: What principles guide your decisions? These should be in harmony with your target market's expectations and always be evident in your actions.

A clear purpose and set of values will forge a strong emotional bond with your audience, ensuring they remain loyal to your brand over time.

2. Maintaining Consistency

For influence and lasting value to materialize, your brand must exhibit consistency at every touchpoint, from customer service to marketing. The wealthy understand that consistency fosters recognition and trust.

- **Visual Identity**: Ensure your logo, color palette, and fonts stay uniform across all platforms.
- **Tone of Voice**: Keep your communication style consistent to reflect your brand's personality.
- **Customer Experience**: Deliver a seamless and exceptional customer experience consistently across all interactions.

As I shared in *The Unstoppable Road to Wealth Creation*, consistency in branding is essential for gaining trust and recognition, which leads to long-term influence.

3. Delivering Value with Content

In the digital age, content is king. A strong brand does not simply sell products or services but offers value through education, inspiration, and entertainment.

- **Educational Content**: Offer resources that help customers make better financial or purchasing decisions. This establishes you as an authority.

- **Inspirational Engagement**: Create content that speaks to your audience emotionally. Whether through social media, blogs, or video, ensure your content tells a story that resonates.

As stated in *The Unstoppable Road to Wealth Creation*, successful branding isn't just about making sales—it's about forming connections and leaving a lasting impact.

The Power of Influence

Influence, much like branding, plays a crucial role in business growth. While building a strong brand is important, establishing influence amplifies your efforts and propels your business to new heights. Influence is the power to shape perceptions, inspire action, and create meaningful change. The wealthy often leverage their influence to broaden their reach and enhance their brand.

1. Becoming a Thought Leader

Thought leaders have the ability to shape industries, create trends, and define the future. By positioning yourself as a thought leader, you gain not only influence but also the opportunity to attract partnerships, investment prospects, and business expansion.

- **Publishing Articles**: Share your expertise through books, blogs, and articles.
- **Speaking Engagements**: Attend and speak at events to demonstrate your authority.
- **Showcasing Success Stories**: Share examples of your business's success to build credibility.

As noted in *The Unstoppable Road to Wealth Creation*, establishing yourself as a leader in your field requires a long-term commitment to showcasing your expertise and value.

2. Networking and Building Strong Relationships

The wealthy understand that influence extends beyond personal reputation—it's also about who you connect with. Networking with influential individuals opens doors to collaborations, investments, and growth opportunities.

- **Strategic Partnerships**: Collaborate with businesses and people who share similar values and can help elevate your brand.
- **Seek Mentorship**: Connect with mentors who can provide guidance on scaling your influence and making strategic decisions.
- **Engage with Influencers**: Collaborate with influencers who can help expand your brand's visibility.

Building influential relationships and aligning with key players in your industry can significantly enhance your brand's reach and influence.

3. Leveraging Social Media for Influence

In today's digital world, social media is one of the most powerful platforms for expanding your influence. The wealthy have mastered using digital channels to strengthen their brand and attract a loyal following.

- **Social Media Strategy**: Engage on platforms like LinkedIn, Instagram, Twitter, and TikTok to reach your audience and grow your brand.
- **Personal Branding**: Share your experiences and stories to establish your personal brand and influence.

As highlighted in *The Unstoppable Road to Wealth Creation*, digital platforms offer unique opportunities to quickly grow your influence and reach a global audience.

Avoiding Common Branding Pitfalls

While branding and influence are powerful, they must be carefully managed to avoid damage. Here are some common mistakes to avoid:

1. **Lack of Clarity** – A confusing brand is easily forgotten. Be clear about what your brand stands for.
2. **Inconsistent Messaging** – Inconsistent branding can cause confusion and erode trust.
3. **Failure to Adapt** – A brand that doesn't evolve risks becoming outdated.
4. **Ignoring Customer Feedback** – Brands that don't listen to their audience risk losing relevance.

Conclusion: Building Lasting Value Through Branding and Influence

Branding and influence are not merely tools for business expansion—they are the foundation for creating lasting wealth and value. As I discuss in *The Unstoppable Road to Wealth Creation*, wealthy individuals don't just create businesses; they develop brands that connect deeply with their customers, inspire loyalty, and create enduring legacies.

By developing a solid, authentic brand and harnessing influence, you can position yourself as an industry leader, unlock opportunities for wealth-building, and leave a lasting impact that transcends your lifetime.

In the next chapter, we'll explore how to master time management which is how the wealthy maximize productivity.

CHAPTER 15: MASTERING TIME MANAGEMENT – HOW THE WEALTHY MAXIMIZE PRODUCTIVITY

Introduction

Time is an irreplaceable asset. Unlike money, which can be earned and multiplied, time is finite. Wealthy individuals understand that how they manage their time directly affects their success. This chapter explores how the wealthy optimize their time, delegate effectively, and use strategic thinking to maximize their productivity and results. As Napoleon Hill said in *Think and Grow Rich*: "The way of success is the way of continuous pursuit of knowledge." The wealthy treat time as their most precious resource, constantly seeking opportunities to learn, grow, and create.

1. The Wealthy Think in Terms of Time Investment

The rich don't view time as a set number of hours; they see it in terms of returns on time investment (ROTI).

- **Poor mindset:** Works for a fixed wage per hour.
- **Wealthy mindset:** Focuses on high-value tasks that yield exponential returns.
- **Example:** A successful entrepreneur might spend their time securing a million-dollar investment instead of handling everyday operations.

Quote from The Science of Getting Rich: "The very best thing you can do for the whole world is to make the most of yourself." – Wallace D. Wattles

2. The 80/20 Rule (Pareto Principle) – Prioritization

The wealthy apply the 80/20 Rule, which states that 80% of results come from just 20% of efforts.

- They eliminate distractions and prioritize high-impact activities.
- **Example:** A business owner might prioritize securing important partnerships while outsourcing routine administrative work.
- **Steve Jobs:** Known for eliminating unnecessary projects to focus on groundbreaking innovations.

3. Delegation and Outsourcing – Leveraging Others' Time

The wealthy recognize they cannot do everything alone, so they delegate tasks to free up their time for higher-value activities.

- **Business Owners:** Hire employees or virtual assistants to manage operational tasks.
- **Investors:** Rely on financial advisors to manage their portfolios while focusing on strategy.

- **Example:** Jeff Bezos built Amazon by delegating logistics and operations so he could concentrate on growth strategies.

Quote from Robert Greene, The 48 Laws of Power: "Never waste valuable time, or mental peace of mind, on the affairs of others—that is too high a price to pay."

4. Creating Systems Instead of Manual Work

The wealthy avoid repetitive tasks by creating automated systems.

- **Example:** Instead of handling customer service directly, a company may use an AI chatbot.
- **Investor Strategy:** Set up passive income streams like dividends or real estate to create wealth without constant effort.
- **Business Strategy:** Franchise models, such as McDonald's, allow wealth generation without the founder's constant involvement.

5. The Power of Saying NO

Warren Buffett once said: "The difference between successful people and very successful people is that very successful people say no to almost everything."

- The wealthy guard their time by turning down distractions, unimportant meetings, and energy-draining activities.
- **Example:** Elon Musk avoids unnecessary meetings and focuses only on critical decision-making at Tesla and SpaceX.

6. The Daily Routines of the Wealthy

Wealthy individuals structure their days to maximize efficiency.

- **Morning Routines:** Many begin their day with exercise, meditation, reading, and planning.

- **Focused Work Periods:** Set specific hours for deep, uninterrupted work.
- **Reflection and Learning:** Dedicate time for personal growth and learning.

Examples of Routines:

- **Oprah Winfrey:** Starts her day with meditation and gratitude exercises.
- **Mark Zuckerberg:** Wears the same outfit every day to reduce decision fatigue.
- **Elon Musk:** Divides his day into 5-minute time blocks to maximize efficiency.

7. Mastering Time Blocks and Deep Work

The wealthy use time blocking to focus on high-priority tasks.

- **Example:** Bill Gates schedules "Think Weeks" where he isolates himself to focus on innovation.
- **Deep Work (Cal Newport's Concept):** Avoid distractions to produce high-quality work in shorter periods.
- **Pomodoro Technique:** 25-minute work intervals followed by short breaks help maintain focus.

8. How to Master Time Like the Wealthy

1. **Identify high-value tasks** – Focus on activities that offer the highest returns.
2. **Eliminate low-impact activities** – Avoid excessive social media, unnecessary meetings, and unproductive habits.
3. **Use a structured calendar** – Plan your day ahead and dedicate time blocks for important tasks.
4. **Delegate and automate** – Invest in tools, software, and people to handle routine tasks.

5. **Develop a morning routine** – Start your day with clarity and purpose.
6. **Review and reflect daily** – Constantly assess how you're spending your time and make adjustments.

Conclusion: Time as the Ultimate Wealth Multiplier

Wealthy individuals understand that how they manage their time shapes their success. By prioritizing, delegating, creating systems, and sticking to solid routines, they optimize their productivity and impact.

Key Takeaways:

✅ Time is your most valuable asset.

✅ Wealthy individuals focus on high-value tasks.

✅ Delegation and automation free up time for growth.

✅ Successful people avoid distractions.

✅ A structured routine leads to long-term success.

By mastering time management, you can enhance your productivity, achieve financial success, and live a well-balanced life. In the next chapter, we will dive into how the wealthy leverage negotiation and persuasion to gain an edge in business and life.

CHAPTER 16: THE ART OF NEGOTIATION AND PASUASION – HOW THE WEALTHY GET WHAT THEY WANT

Introduction

Negotiation is a key driver of wealth creation. Whether in business, investments, or everyday interactions, the ability to persuade and negotiate effectively can determine financial success or failure. Wealthy individuals understand the psychology behind influence, master strategic communication, and apply proven principles to secure favourable outcomes in every deal. As Robert Greene explains in *The 48 Laws of Power*: "Persuasion is about creating desire in others to act in your favour while making them think it was their own choice." This chapter delves into the negotiation tactics of the rich and powerful, providing insights on how you can apply these strategies to achieve success.

1. The Wealthy Always Negotiate

The wealthy never accept the initial offer; they negotiate everything. Whether buying a property, finalizing a business deal, or signing contracts, they know that every transaction is up for negotiation.

- **Example:** Billionaire investor Warren Buffett is known for negotiating deals that provide him with the best terms, often securing long-term benefits.
- **Scenario:** A real estate investor negotiating the price of a property doesn't settle for the asking price but uses market knowledge and financial positioning to secure better terms.

Quote from The Science of Getting Rich: "You must always look for the advantage in every transaction, for it is the way of the truly wealthy." – Wallace D. Wattles

2. Mastering Persuasion

The wealthy are exceptional at persuasion. They know how to frame conversations, use silence strategically, and appeal to emotions to influence others.

- **The Rule of Reciprocity:** When you offer something to others, they feel compelled to return the favor.
    - **Example:** A business owner gives free, valuable advice before asking for a partnership.
- **The Contrast Principle:** Presenting a high-priced option first makes subsequent offers appear more reasonable.
    - **Example:** A salesperson shows an expensive item first, then presents a more affordable one, making the second option seem like a great deal.

Quote from Think and Grow Rich: "The ability to influence people without irritating them is one of the most valuable skills a person can possess." – Napoleon Hill

3. Using Leverage in Negotiations

Wealthy individuals understand the power of leverage—having something the other party wants and using it to their advantage.

- They strive for win-win situations but ensure they benefit the most.
- **Example:** A tech entrepreneur negotiating funding for their startup offers investors equity, but only under terms that allow them to retain control over the company.
- **Scenario:** In a salary negotiation, rather than just asking for a raise, you highlight your unique skills, accomplishments, and the value you bring to the company, making it harder for your employer to refuse.

Quote from The Art of Money Getting: "The wealthiest individuals are those who learn to use circumstances to their benefit rather than complain about them." – P.T. Barnum

4. The Power of Walking Away

One of the greatest negotiation strengths is knowing when to walk away.

- Wealthy individuals never act out of desperation during a deal.
- If the terms aren't favorable, they confidently step back, knowing that other opportunities will arise.
- **Example:** Jeff Bezos walked away from an early business deal that would have cost him equity in Amazon, waiting for a better opportunity.

5. Emotional Control and Strategic Silence

The wealthy maintain composure and patience during negotiations.

- Silence is a powerful tool—people often become uncomfortable with it and may concede more just to fill the gap.
- **Scenario:** In a salary negotiation, remaining silent after stating your desired amount forces the employer to justify their response instead of immediately countering.

Quote from The 48 Laws of Power: "The more you say, the more likely you are to say something foolish." – Robert Greene

6. Practical Steps to Negotiate Like the Wealthy

1. **Do Your Research** – Understand market value, the other party's motivations, and gather facts before negotiating.
2. **Be Prepared to Walk Away** – Never negotiate out of desperation.
3. **Use Silence Effectively** – Let the other party reveal more than they intended.
4. **Create Win-Win Scenarios** – Frame your deals as mutually beneficial while ensuring you come out on top.
5. **Leverage Emotional Triggers** – Use reciprocity, urgency, and contrast to influence decisions.
6. **Be Confident and Assertive** – Speak with authority, knowing that you bring value to the table.

Conclusion: Negotiation is the Key to Wealth

Wealthy individuals understand that everything is negotiable. They don't settle for average deals—they create opportunities that work in their favour. By applying these strategies, you can improve your financial outcomes, enhance your business deals, and build long-term wealth.

Key Takeaways:

✅ Always negotiate—never accept the first offer.

✅ Master persuasion and leverage emotions.

✅ Use silence and emotional control to your advantage.

✅ Walk away when necessary—desperation weakens your position.

✅ Negotiate like the wealthy to build lasting financial success.

In the next chapter, we will explore the significance of branding and influence—how the wealthy build and maintain their powerful personal and business brands.

CHAPTER 17: BUILDING STRATEGIC PARTNERSHIPS – THE RICH NEVER WORK ALONE

Introduction

In the world of wealth creation, success rarely happens in isolation. Wealthy individuals understand that collaboration is a powerful tool. Strategic partnerships open doors to resources, opportunities, and expertise that one individual cannot access alone. In this chapter, we'll explore the importance of building meaningful partnerships and how the wealthy use these relationships to expand their influence and achieve lasting success.

As mentioned in *The Unstoppable Road to Wealth Creation*, wealth creation is not a solitary journey but a networked endeavour, where collaboration often paves the path to greater achievements. Successful individuals understand that surrounding themselves with the right people can propel them towards their goals faster than going it alone.

1. The Power of Collaboration

Wealthy individuals recognize that their success is often a result of collaborating with others who bring complementary skills, knowledge, and networks to the table. These collaborations can range from business partnerships to personal connections that help accelerate growth.

Example: Bill Gates and Paul Allen's partnership at Microsoft showcases how two individuals with complementary skills can build a billion-dollar company. Gates' technical knowledge combined with Allen's vision and business acumen created a thriving empire.

Reference from *The Unstoppable Road to Wealth Creation*: In my book, I emphasized that "Partnerships are the shortcuts that help you leverage your time, skills, and resources. You can't reach new heights alone; it's the collective power of shared wisdom and effort that makes the difference."

2. Leveraging Expertise Through Partnerships

Strategic partnerships allow the wealthy to tap into expertise they don't have. Instead of trying to master everything themselves, they form alliances with those who have specialized knowledge, thus allowing them to make more informed decisions and avoid costly mistakes.

Example: Warren Buffett's partnerships with Charlie Munger are a prime example of leveraging expertise. Buffett's investment acumen combined with Munger's legal and business knowledge has enabled them to grow Berkshire Hathaway into one of the most successful companies in history.

Reference from *The Unstoppable Road to Wealth Creation*: In my book, I discuss how "The value of a partnership lies in the expertise that each party brings. By building relationships with experts, you reduce your own risk while enhancing your ability to execute your vision."

3. Creating Win-Win Relationships

A key principle of successful partnerships is creating win-win situations, where both parties benefit. The wealthy approach partnerships with a mindset of mutual benefit, ensuring that both sides gain from the collaboration.

Example: The partnership between Richard Branson and Niklas Zennström, co-founder of Skype, led to the growth of multiple ventures. Branson's Virgin Group supported Skype's expansion, and in return, he benefited from the rapid growth and exposure that Skype offered.

Reference from *The Unstoppable Road to Wealth Creation*: In my book, I emphasized that "When negotiating partnerships, always focus on mutual benefits. A successful partnership is one where both parties are empowered and feel valued, leading to sustained collaboration."

4. Expanding Your Network

The wealthy often build partnerships with influential individuals who can introduce them to new opportunities. This includes not only business connections but also strategic relationships that provide access to new markets, investments, and exclusive deals.

Example: Oprah Winfrey's relationship with her mentor, Maya Angelou, opened doors for Oprah in her career and allowed her to navigate the media industry with wisdom and confidence.

Reference from *The Unstoppable Road to Wealth Creation*: One of the key strategies I discussed in my book was the importance of "networking with purpose." By aligning yourself with the right people, you position yourself in a way that opens up new avenues for growth and opportunity, which accelerates your journey toward wealth.

5. Navigating Challenges Together

Partnerships help individuals navigate challenges and risks more effectively. Wealthy people often view setbacks as learning opportunities within the context of their partnerships, working together to find solutions rather than facing challenges alone.

Example: Steve Jobs and Steve Wozniak faced many obstacles while building Apple, but their ability to collaborate and complement each other's strengths helped them overcome these challenges and create one of the most valuable companies in the world.

Reference from *The Unstoppable Road to Wealth Creation*: In my book, I mentioned that "challenges will inevitably arise, but partnerships provide a support system that makes tackling adversity less daunting. Strong partners provide a cushion, allowing you to move forward even when obstacles appear."

6. Building Partnerships for Long-Term Success

Successful individuals understand the importance of cultivating partnerships for long-term sustainability. The focus is not on short-term gains but on nurturing relationships that will continue to bear fruit in the future.

Example: Jeff Bezos' relationship with early investors such as Venture Capital firms led to the rapid growth of Amazon, but Bezos' focus on maintaining these long-term relationships allowed Amazon to continuously innovate and expand.

Reference from *The Unstoppable Road to Wealth Creation*: I discuss in my book how "long-term success isn't just about making deals today, but ensuring that the relationships you form today will yield benefits in the years to come. Think beyond immediate gains and focus on sustainable growth."

7. How You Can Build Strategic Partnerships

1. **Identify Synergies** – Look for individuals or businesses that complement your strengths and fill gaps in your knowledge or resources.
2. **Offer Value First** – The best partnerships are built on trust and mutual respect. Offer value to your potential partners before seeking something in return.
3. **Be Transparent and Honest** – Open communication is essential in building trust and a strong partnership.
4. **Focus on Shared Goals** – Ensure that both parties have aligned objectives and that the partnership will lead to mutual growth.
5. **Invest in the Relationship** – Partnerships require ongoing nurturing. Be willing to invest time and resources into making the relationship work.

Conclusion: The Collective Power of Partnerships

Building strategic partnerships is one of the most effective ways to create wealth. The wealthy understand that working alone limits their potential. By forming the right partnerships, they multiply their efforts, leverage external resources, and expand their reach. As emphasized in *The Unstoppable Road to Wealth Creation*, creating a powerful network and building partnerships is integral to sustaining long-term success.

Key Takeaways:

✅ Strategic partnerships accelerate growth and provide access to new resources.

✅ Leverage expertise, share benefits, and create long-term relationships.

✅ Surround yourself with individuals who can enhance your strengths and help mitigate weaknesses.

✅ Networking with purpose positions you for success in the long run.

✅ A successful partnership provides shared benefits and growth opportunities for both sides.

By following the strategies outlined in this chapter and aligning yourself with the right people, you can build powerful partnerships that will help propel you toward lasting wealth and success.

PART 4:

MASTERING WEALTH FOR LIFE

CHAPTER 18: THE SECRETS OF ULTRA-WEALTHY FAMILIES AND THEIR STRATEGIES FOR FINANCIAL DOMINANCE

Introduction

Wealthy families don't sustain their financial power by chance. Their lasting success results from careful planning, smart investments, disciplined financial management, and the ability to adapt across generations. These families implement proven wealth-building principles that ensure their financial legacy not only endures but grows over time.

As Napoleon Hill famously said in *Think and Grow Rich*: *"The ladder of success is never crowded at the top."*

This chapter uncovers the hidden financial strategies that ultra-wealthy families use and how you can apply them to secure generational wealth.

1. Establishing Multi-Generational Wealth Structures

Affluent families recognize that without proper financial systems in place, wealth can quickly disappear. A study by Williams Group Wealth Consultancy found that 70% of wealthy families lose their fortune by the second generation, and 90% by the third. To prevent this, the ultra-rich implement structured financial frameworks.

How They Preserve Wealth:

✅ **Family Trusts & Foundations** – These safeguard assets against taxation, legal claims, and poor financial decisions.
✅ **Family Offices** – Private firms that manage a family's entire financial portfolio, ensuring long-term wealth protection.
✅ **Succession & Governance Plans** – Clear guidelines to control inheritance and ensure a smooth transition of wealth.

Example: The Rothschild family has sustained financial dominance for over 250 years by maintaining private banking systems, diversifying investments, and implementing well-structured financial plans.

🔹 **Key Takeaway:** Use legal frameworks to protect and manage wealth efficiently for future generations.

📖 **Quote:**
"A good person leaves an inheritance for their children's children." — Proverbs 13:22

2. Prioritizing Ownership of Appreciating Assets

Instead of relying solely on income, ultra-wealthy families focus on accumulating assets that gain value over time.

📌 **Real Estate** – Investing in income-generating properties that appreciate in value.

📌 **Business Ownership & Private Equity** – Controlling companies rather than just working for them.
📌 **Stocks & Dividends** – Investing in shares that provide long-term growth and passive income.
📌 **Intellectual Property & Royalties** – Earning from patents, books, music, and creative assets.

Example: The Walton family, which owns Walmart, continues to grow their fortune through stock dividends and business ownership.

🔹 **Key Takeaway:** Shift focus from earning wages to acquiring income-generating assets that build long-term wealth.

📖 **Quote:**
"Don't work for money, make money work for you." — Robert Kiyosaki

3. Leveraging the Power of Compound Growth

Albert Einstein called compound interest the "eighth wonder of the world," stating:
"He who understands it, earns it… he who doesn't, pays it."

Ultra-wealthy families reinvest their earnings, allowing their money to multiply over time.

Example: Warren Buffett began investing as a child, and thanks to compounding, over 90% of his fortune was built after his 60s.

🔹 **Key Takeaway:** The earlier you start investing, the more time your money has to grow exponentially.

📖 **Quote:**
"My wealth has come from a combination of living in America, some lucky genes, and compound interest." — Warren Buffett

4. Protecting Wealth Through Legal and Tax Strategies

Preserving wealth is just as crucial as creating it. The ultra-rich use legal and financial strategies to minimize taxes and shield assets from risks.

📖 **Quote:**
"The hardest thing to understand in the world is the income tax." — Albert Einstein

🔹 **Tax Efficiency** – Using trusts, tax-exempt investments, and charitable donations to lower tax burdens.
🔹 **Asset Protection Trusts** – Preventing wealth loss due to lawsuits or poor management.
🔹 **Global Wealth Diversification** – Spreading assets across countries to mitigate financial risks.

🔹 **Key Takeaway:** Utilize tax-efficient strategies to retain more of your wealth and protect it from unnecessary losses.

5. Owning and Controlling Businesses

One of the most significant wealth-building secrets of affluent families is owning businesses rather than just working in them.

📖 **Quote:**
"If you don't find a way to make money while you sleep, you will work until you die." — Warren Buffett

🔹 **Key Takeaway:** Instead of exchanging time for money, build systems that generate wealth independently.

6. Prioritizing Financial Education for Future Generations

One of the primary reasons wealth disappears after a few generations is a lack of financial literacy.

📖 **Quote:**
"Formal education will make you a living; self-education will make you a fortune."
— Jim Rohn

◆ **Key Takeaway:** Teach financial literacy from an early age to ensure wealth is preserved and grown.

7. Thinking in Centuries, Not Just Decades

Ultra-wealthy families plan for financial sustainability over centuries rather than short-term gains.

📖 **Quote:**
"The rich invest in time, the poor invest in money." — Warren Buffett

◆ **Key Takeaway:** Instead of focusing only on immediate financial goals, create a long-term wealth-building strategy that spans multiple generations.

Conclusion: Apply These Principles to Secure Your Financial Future

The ultra-wealthy follow unique financial habits that set them apart. They plan meticulously, invest wisely, protect their assets, and educate their heirs.

📖 Final Quotes for Reflection:

◆ *"The secret to wealth is simple: Find a way to do more for others than anyone else does. Become more valuable. Do more. Give more. Be more. Serve more."* — Tony Robbins

◆ *"No man can become rich without himself enriching others."* — Andrew Carnegie

◆ *"The only thing that interferes with my learning is my education."* — Albert Einstein

By implementing these strategies, you can build wealth that lasts for generations.

CHAPTER 19: THE POWER OF MENTORSHIP AND LEARNING FROM THE WEALTHY

Introduction

"Surround yourself with people who are only going to lift you higher." — Oprah Winfrey.

When you examine the lives of the wealthiest and most successful individuals throughout history, one thing is clear: they all had mentors. Success leaves behind clues, and those who accumulate great wealth often do so by learning from those who have already navigated the path.

Mentorship serves as a shortcut to success—offering direct access to wisdom, experience, and opportunities that could take years, if not decades, to accumulate on your own. The wealthiest people recognize that investing in knowledge and relationships is the key to growth.

In this chapter, we'll delve into how mentorship, learning from the wealthy, and strategic networking can significantly speed up your journey to financial success. Additionally, we'll explore historical examples and real-life stories that showcase the transformative power of mentorship.

1. The Wealthy Always Seek Mentors

🕮 Quote:

"If I have seen further, it is by standing on the shoulders of giants."
— Isaac Newton

The wealthiest individuals did not achieve success in isolation. They actively sought out mentors who provided guidance, helped them avoid costly mistakes, and opened doors to life-changing opportunities.

Examples of Wealthy People Who Had Mentors:

✅ **Warren Buffett & Benjamin Graham** – Buffett, one of the world's wealthiest investors, credits much of his success to his mentor, Benjamin Graham, the father of value investing. Graham's principles on financial discipline and long-term wealth-building shaped Buffett's approach.

✅ **Bill Gates & Warren Buffett** – Gates, Microsoft's co-founder, has mentioned that his relationship with Buffett significantly impacted his approach to business, philanthropy, and long-term vision.

✅ **Oprah Winfrey & Maya Angelou** – Oprah often acknowledges that poet and mentor Maya Angelou played a key role in shaping her success, especially in developing confidence and purpose.

✅ **Andrew Carnegie & Napoleon Hill** – Steel magnate Andrew Carnegie personally mentored Napoleon Hill, who went on to write *Think and Grow Rich*, a highly influential book on wealth creation.

◆ **Lesson:** The wealthiest people understand that by learning from experienced mentors, they reduce the risks of trial and error, accelerating their path to success.

2. Learning from the Wealthy – The Power of Modeling Success

📖 Quote:
"Your income is determined by your philosophy, not by the economy." — Jim Rohn
One of the most effective ways to build wealth is to learn from the behaviors, habits, and principles of the rich. This is why successful individuals read books, attend seminars, and actively seek financial education.

Key Lessons from the Wealthy:

✓ **Long-Term Thinking** – The wealthy think decades ahead, focusing on long-term growth rather than immediate gratification.
✓ **Investing in Assets** – They prioritize assets like real estate, stocks, and businesses that generate passive income.
✓ **Time Over Money** – Wealthy individuals delegate tasks, allowing them to focus on high-impact activities.
✓ **Networking** – Building and expanding a network is a priority for wealthy individuals, as relationships often unlock wealth-building opportunities.

📖 **Example:**
• **Elon Musk** drew inspiration from historical figures such as Thomas Edison and Nikola Tesla, learning from their work and applying their innovative ideas to modern industries like space exploration and electric vehicles.

🔷 **Lesson:** To build wealth, study those who have already achieved success—whether through books, interviews, or direct mentorship.

3. Personal Case Study – How Mentorship Changed My Life

In my own journey of wealth creation, one of the most pivotal decisions I made was seeking mentorship from those who had already found success. Early in my career, I discovered:

✅ **Learning Solo Was Slow** – Figuring everything out alone was frustrating and time-consuming.

✅ **Mistakes Were Costly** – Mistakes that cost me thousands could have been avoided with guidance.

✅ **Mentorship Opened Doors** – Mentors not only offered valuable knowledge but also introduced me to influential connections.

📖 Example from My Experience:

Early on, I met an accomplished entrepreneur who taught me how to leverage other people's expertise. He stressed that "Your network is your net worth." Because of this advice, I was able to:

- Avoid common mistakes many first-time entrepreneurs make.
- Structure my business for long-term success.
- Master negotiation and deal-making, which allowed me to secure better contracts.

🔷 **Lesson:** Mentorship saves time, money, and effort by helping you avoid costly mistakes and providing direct access to valuable knowledge.

4. The Wealthy Build Strategic Networks

📖 Quote:

"Your network is your net worth." — Porter Gale

The wealthy don't just seek mentorship—they intentionally build powerful networks that propel their success. They understand that having access to the right people is often more valuable than money.

How to Build a Wealthy Network:

✅ **Attend High-Value Events** – Conferences, mastermind groups, and investment summits provide opportunities to meet influential individuals.
✅ **Offer Value First** – Instead of asking for favours, focus on how you can help successful people.
✅ **Leverage Social Media** – Platforms like LinkedIn, Twitter, and Clubhouse can connect you with industry leaders.
✅ **Be in the Right Rooms** – Surround yourself with people who challenge and inspire you.

📖 **Example:**
• **Mark Zuckerberg** expanded Facebook by networking with investors like Peter Thiel and other Silicon Valley leaders, turning the platform from a college project into a global empire.

🔹 **Lesson:** Who you know can be just as valuable as what you know when it comes to building wealth.

6. Actionable Steps to Find the Right Mentor and Network

📖 Quote:
"Success is neither magical nor mysterious. Success is the natural consequence of consistently applying basic fundamentals." — Jim Rohn.

To build wealth through mentorship and networking, follow these steps:

1 **Identify Your Ideal Mentor** – Look for someone who has achieved what you want to accomplish.

2 **Invest in Relationships** – Join masterminds, networking groups, and mentorship programs.

3 **Offer Value First** – Focus on providing value before asking for anything in return.

4 **Be a Lifelong Learner** – Continually educate yourself through books, seminars, and self-improvement.

5 **Take Action on Advice** – A mentor's guidance is only valuable if you put it into practice.

📖 Example:

• **Tony Robbins** sought mentorship from Jim Rohn, and through that relationship, he built a multi-million-dollar empire helping others achieve success.

◆ **Lesson:** Mentorship is only valuable if you apply what you learn to your life and business.

Conclusion: Success Leaves Clues – Follow the Wealthy

Key Takeaways:

✅ Mentorship is a shortcut to success—learn from those who've already succeeded.

✅ The wealthy constantly study other wealthy individuals—success leaves behind clues.

✅ Your network determines your net worth—surround yourself with high-value individuals.

✅ Model successful strategies from those who have already achieved greatness.

✅ Apply the knowledge you gain—knowledge without action is wasted.

📖 **Final Quote:**
"Formal education will make you a living; self-education will make you a fortune." — Jim Rohn

🚀 Final Lesson:

To build massive wealth, find the right mentors, study successful people, and expand your network. The knowledge and connections you gain will pay off far more than any financial investment.

CHAPTER 20: THE POWER OF PATIENCE IN WEALTH CREATION

Introduction

"Patience, persistence, and effort form an unstoppable trio for success." — Napoleon Hill.

Accumulating wealth is a long-term endeavour, much like a marathon rather than a sprint. The most successful individuals recognize that financial prosperity demands patience, discipline, and strategic thinking. Many people seek instant riches, but those who establish enduring wealth embrace long-term planning, delayed gratification, and calculated decision-making.

In this chapter, we will explore:

✅ The critical role of patience in financial growth

✅ Notable historical figures who benefited from patience

✅ A personal experience demonstrating patience in wealth creation
✅ Actionable techniques to cultivate financial patience

1. Wealth Accumulates Over Time, Not Overnight

📖 *"The stock market is a mechanism for transferring wealth from the impatient to the patient."* — Warren Buffett

Wealthy individuals understand that building financial stability takes time. Whether through investing, business development, or asset management, they stay committed to long-term objectives.

Historical Example: Warren Buffett – The Patient Investor

✅ Began investing at age 11 but did not amass wealth overnight.
✅ Held investments for decades, allowing compound interest to work in his favor.
✅ Avoided high-risk, impulsive financial decisions, focusing instead on steady, long-term gains.
🔹 **Lesson:** Sustainable wealth comes from patience, strategic investing, and time.

2. Personal Experience – The Power of Patience in My Financial Journey

Early in my entrepreneurial journey, I sought immediate financial rewards, only to realize that real success stems from patience, perseverance, and consistency.
✅ Instead of seeking quick profits, I prioritized long-term business growth.
✅ I reinvested my earnings rather than indulging in unnecessary expenses.

✅ Over time, disciplined actions compounded, leading to financial stability.

📖 **Reference from My Book (The Unstoppable Road to Wealth Creation):**
In *The Unstoppable Road to Wealth Creation*, I highlight that patience distinguishes short-lived success from lasting wealth. Knowing when to wait and resist fleeting trends is a critical financial skill.

🔹 **Lesson:** The most successful individuals see patience as an essential component of their financial strategy.

3. The Common Pitfall – Why Many Fail Due to Impatience

📖 *"Extraordinary results come from simple, consistent actions over time."* — Warren Buffett

Many people struggle to build wealth due to:
❌ A desire for immediate success and fast money.
❌ Abandoning financial goals when challenges arise.
❌ Lack of patience in allowing investments and businesses to mature.
❌ Constantly shifting from one venture to another without giving them time to flourish.

📖 **Example:**

- Studies reveal that over 90% of traders lose money because they seek quick gains instead of long-term growth.
- Conversely, patient investors who hold stocks for years see substantial returns.

  🔹 **Lesson:** True financial success requires patience, discipline, and a commitment to long-term vision.

4. The Magic of Compound Interest – The Ultimate Reward for Patience

🕮 *"Compound interest is the eighth wonder of the world. Those who understand it, earn it... those who don't, pay it."* — Albert Einstein

One of the most powerful examples of patience in wealth creation is compound interest.

Example: Investing Early and Waiting

✅ Person A invests $200 per month from ages 25 to 35 and then stops.

✅ Person B starts investing $200 per month at age 35 and continues until age 65.
Despite investing for only ten years, Person A ends up with more wealth than Person B, thanks to compound interest.

🔹 **Lesson:** The earlier you start and the longer you remain patient, the greater your financial gains.

5. How to Strengthen Your Financial Patience

🕮 *"Great things come to those who wait, but only what's left by those who act."* — Abraham Lincoln

To develop financial patience, try these exercises:

Exercise 1: The One-Year Investment Challenge

✅ Invest a set amount in stocks, real estate, or business ventures.

✅ Do not withdraw funds for at least a year.

✅ Observe how patience leads to wealth accumulation.

Exercise 2: Monitor Progress Periodically

✅ Set financial goals and review progress every six months.

✅ Avoid checking investments daily to prevent impulsive decisions.

Exercise 3: Delay Gratification for Bigger Gains

✅ Instead of buying luxury items immediately, allocate funds for investments.

✅ Build financial discipline by resisting unnecessary expenses.

🔹 **Lesson:** Patience in financial decisions leads to significant long-term rewards.

6. The Wealthy Remain Committed to the Process

📖 *"Time in the market beats timing the market."* — Peter Lynch

The ultra-wealthy adhere to their financial plans, regardless of short-term fluctuations.

Example: Jeff Bezos and Amazon

✅ Launched Amazon in 1994, enduring years of losses before becoming profitable.

✅ Faced skepticism but stayed patient and focused.

✅ Today, Amazon is a global powerhouse.

🔹 **Lesson:** Success belongs to those who trust the process and remain patient.

Conclusion: Patience is the Secret to Wealth

💡 Key Takeaways:

✅ Wealth accumulation is a long-term process.

✅ The impatient often lose money, while the patient steadily grow their wealth.

✅ Compound interest rewards those who wait.

✅ Successful entrepreneurs and investors stay dedicated to their

long-term goals.
✅ Practical exercises can help cultivate financial patience.

📖 **Final Quote:**
"The secret of getting ahead is getting started. The secret of getting started is breaking overwhelming tasks into small, manageable steps and tackling the first one." — Mark Twain

🚀 Final Lesson:

To build lasting wealth, cultivate the patience to allow investments, businesses, and financial strategies to mature. History's wealthiest individuals did not rush success—they leveraged the power of time and patience.

CHAPTER 21: THE POWER OF SELF-DISCIPLINE – THE WEALTHY MASTER THEMSELVES BEFORE MASTERING WEALTH

Introduction

"Self-discipline is the bridge between goals and accomplishment." — Jim Rohn

One key trait shared by the world's most successful and wealthy individuals is self-discipline. Wealth isn't created overnight, nor is it sustained without unwavering effort, control, and focus. The ability to delay gratification, remain committed, and consistently execute long-term strategies is what sets the ultra-successful apart from those who struggle financially.

In this chapter, we will examine:

✅ The critical role self-discipline plays in wealth creation.

✅ Real-life examples of self-disciplined individuals.

✅ Practical strategies to cultivate and strengthen self-discipline.

1. The Connection Between Self-Discipline and Wealth

📖 Quote: "If you do not conquer self, you will be conquered by self." — Napoleon Hill, *Think and Grow Rich*

Many people fail to achieve financial success, not due to a lack of knowledge, but because they lack discipline. Wealthy individuals train themselves to:

✅ Resist unnecessary expenses.

✅ Adhere to long-term financial plans.

✅ Work consistently, even when unmotivated.

✅ Stay focused on their objectives despite distractions.

Example: Warren Buffett – A Master of Financial Discipline

✅ Despite his vast fortune, Buffett continues to live in the same modest house he purchased in 1958.

✅ He prioritizes calculated, long-term investments over impulsive decisions.

✅ He dedicates hours daily to reading and analysing financial markets to refine his strategy.

🔹 **Lesson:** Financial success doesn't stem from luck—it results from disciplined, persistent effort over time.

2. Delayed Gratification: A Fundamental Principle of Wealth

📖 Quote: "The ability to discipline yourself to delay gratification is the road to financial success." — Brian Tracy

A defining difference between the wealthy and the financially struggling is how they handle instant gratification. The wealthy understand the importance of sacrificing short-term pleasures for long-term prosperity.

Example: The Marshmallow Experiment

✅ In a well-known study by psychologist Walter Mischel, children were tested on their ability to delay gratification.
✅ Those who resisted the urge to eat a marshmallow immediately, in favor of a greater reward later, were found to achieve more success in adulthood.
✅ This principle applies to wealth creation—individuals who prioritize investing over impulsive spending build lasting financial stability.

◆ **Lesson:** Those who think long-term and exercise patience reap greater financial rewards.

3. How the Wealthy Develop Self-Discipline

📖 Quote: "Success is nothing more than a few simple disciplines, practiced every day." — Jim Rohn

Discipline is not innate—it is cultivated through daily habits.

Key Habits of Financially Disciplined Individuals:

1. **They Set Clear Financial Goals 📌**

   ✅ Wealthy people define specific financial objectives.

   ✅ They break goals into smaller, actionable steps.

2. **They Automate Wealth-Building 💰**

   ✅ Instead of relying on willpower, they set up automatic savings and investments.

   ✅ Their money is allocated to assets before they have the chance to spend it.

3. **They Avoid Impulsive Decisions 🛑**

   ✅ Wealthy individuals do not let emotions dictate financial choices.

   ✅ They conduct thorough research, analyze risks, and think strategically.

4. **They Prioritize Continuous Learning 📖**

   ✅ Successful individuals invest time in reading, learning, and skill-building.

   ✅ Example: Elon Musk reads two books per week to expand his knowledge.

🔹 **Lesson:** Financial success is the result of small, consistent, disciplined actions.

4. Personal Experience – How Discipline Transformed My Financial Journey

At the start of my entrepreneurial journey, I realized that without self-discipline, my financial goals would remain out of reach.

✅ I created and adhered to a strict budget, avoiding unnecessary expenses.
✅ I committed to saving and investing, even when it was

challenging.
✅ I prioritized learning about wealth-building strategies daily.

Over time, these disciplined habits reshaped my financial future.

📖 **Reference from My Book (*The Unstoppable Road to Wealth Creation*)**: In *The Unstoppable Road to Wealth Creation*, I emphasize that strong financial habits create a cycle of success. The wealthy understand that discipline is the foundation of financial growth.

🔹 **Lesson:** Financial success is rooted in disciplined, daily financial habits.

5. Strategies to Develop Unbreakable Financial Discipline

📖 Quote: "A man without decision of character can never be said to belong to himself... He belongs to whatever can make him captive." — Napoleon Hill

If you want to cultivate the self-discipline of the wealthy, follow these steps:

Step 1: Identify Your Weaknesses

✅ Are you prone to overspending? Do you avoid budgeting? Get easily distracted?
✅ Acknowledge these weaknesses so you can address them directly.

Step 2: Establish Financial Rules

✅ Example: Commit to saving at least 20% of your income before spending.
✅ Example: Implement a 24-hour waiting period before making any non-essential purchase.

Step 3: Track Your Progress Daily

✅ Wealthy individuals monitor their spending, investments, and financial goals regularly.

✅ Example: Use apps like Mint, YNAB, or Personal Capital to stay on track.

Step 4: Surround Yourself with Disciplined Individuals

✅ If your social circle consists of reckless spenders, maintaining financial discipline will be difficult.

✅ Seek mentors and role models who exemplify financial prudence.

Step 5: Reward Yourself for Discipline

✅ Discipline doesn't mean deprivation—balance discipline with motivation.

✅ Example: After successfully following a savings plan for six months, reward yourself with a small treat.

6. Historical Example – John D. Rockefeller's Financial Discipline

John D. Rockefeller, history's first billionaire, started with nothing but amassed an empire through unwavering financial discipline.

✅ From a young age, he meticulously tracked every cent he spent.

✅ Even after achieving immense wealth, he continued to live modestly.

✅ Rather than squandering his fortune, he reinvested his earnings strategically.

◆ **Lesson:** Rockefeller's disciplined financial management enabled him to create a legacy of wealth that endures to this day.

Conclusion: Self-Discipline Is the Gateway to Wealth

📖 Final Quote: "Wealth is largely the result of habit." — John Jacob Astor

💡 Key Takeaways from This Chapter:

✅ Wealth is built through consistent, disciplined actions over time.

✅ The wealthy embrace delayed gratification—sacrificing short-term comfort for long-term success.

✅ Financial discipline requires monitoring spending, budgeting wisely, and making calculated investments.

✅ Self-discipline is a skill that can be developed through practice and persistence.

🚀 **Final Lesson:** Your financial success hinges on your ability to control your choices, emotions, and decisions. By mastering discipline, you pave the way to lasting prosperity.

CHAPTER 22: THE WEALTHY THINK IN TERMS OF VALUE, NOT JUST MONEY

Introduction

"Try not to become a man of success, but rather try to become a man of value." — **Albert Einstein**

One of the fundamental principles of wealth creation is recognizing that money is merely a by-product of value. The ultra-wealthy do not focus solely on accumulating wealth; instead, they prioritize creating and delivering value to the world. The more significant the problems they solve, the greater their financial rewards.

In this chapter, we will explore:

✅ The distinction between chasing money and creating value.
✅ How wealthy individuals identify and leverage value.
✅ Historical and contemporary examples of wealth built through value creation.
✅ Practical strategies to adopt a value-driven approach to success.

1. The Wealth Formula: Money is a Reflection of Value

📖 **Quote:**
"The amount of money you earn is directly proportional to the value you provide to others." — Bob Burg, *The Go-Giver*

Many believe that hard work alone leads to financial success. However, wealth flows not to those who simply work hard but to those who solve significant problems and provide exceptional value.

Mindset Shift:

🚫 **Limiting Belief:** "How can I make more money?"
✅ **Wealth Mindset:** "How can I provide more value to others?"
Example: Jeff Bezos and Amazon
✅ Rather than merely selling products, Bezos prioritized customer satisfaction, convenience, and efficiency.
✅ He enhanced the online shopping experience, making it faster, more affordable, and more reliable.
✅ This customer-centric approach transformed Amazon into a trillion-dollar empire and made Bezos one of the world's wealthiest individuals.

🔹 **Lesson:** Money follows value. The more people you serve, the greater your wealth potential.

2. Identifying and Leveraging Value for Wealth Creation

📖 **Quote:**
"Your income is determined by how many people you serve and how well you serve them." — Earl Nightingale

Wealthy individuals recognize that value can take many forms beyond monetary transactions.

Forms of Value Creation:

✅ **Innovation:** Developing ground-breaking products (e.g., Steve Jobs and the iPhone).
✅ **Service Excellence:** Providing exceptional customer experiences (e.g., Ritz-Carlton Hotels).
✅ **Investment Insight:** Identifying and funding high-potential opportunities (e.g., Warren Buffett).
✅ **Education & Influence:** Inspiring and teaching others (e.g., Tony Robbins).

Example: Oprah Winfrey – Creating Value Through Media
✅ Oprah built her empire by delivering meaningful content that educated, inspired, and empowered audiences.
✅ She prioritized impact over income, and wealth followed naturally.
✅ Her media influence transformed her into a multi-billionaire.

🔹 **Lesson:** Wealth is a direct reflection of the value you contribute to others.

3. The Wealthy Solve Problems for the Masses

🕮 **Quote:**
"The secret to wealth is simple: Find a way to serve the many, for service to many leads to greatness." — Jim Rohn

Ultra-wealthy individuals do not focus solely on personal gain—they solve large-scale problems that affect millions.

Examples of Wealth Built Through Problem-Solving:

✅ **Elon Musk (Tesla & SpaceX):** Revolutionized sustainable energy and space travel.
✅ **Mark Zuckerberg (Facebook):** Transformed global communication and networking.
✅ **Henry Ford (Automobiles):** Made cars affordable and redefined transportation.

Personal Story: Shifting from Money-Driven to Value-Driven Thinking

Initially, my focus was on making money quickly, but my efforts lacked lasting success. Everything changed when I shifted my mindset:

✅ Instead of asking, *"How can I make more money?"*, I began asking, *"How can I solve meaningful problems?"*
✅ This shift led to exponential business growth and long-term opportunities.

🔹 **Lesson:** Money is not the goal—it is the result of value creation.

4. Practical Strategies to Adopt a Value-Creation Mindset

📖 **Quote:**
"Money is a scoreboard that ranks how well you're providing value to others." — Grant Cardone

To attract wealth, start prioritizing value creation in everything you do.

Step 1: Identify What People Need

✅ Observe common problems in your industry.

✅ Ask yourself: *"What solutions can I provide?"*

Step 2: Master Your Craft

✅ The wealthy excel at what they do.

✅ Example: Michael Jordan dedicated countless hours to perfecting his basketball skills.

Step 3: Scale Your Value

✅ Start by serving one person well, then expand to millions.

✅ Example: A small bakery can scale through online sales and nationwide shipping.

Step 4: Prioritize Impact Over Income

✅ Wealth is a byproduct, not the main goal.

✅ Ask: *"How can I improve lives through my work?"*

◆ **Lesson:** The greater your value, the more inevitable your financial success.

5. Historical Example: Andrew Carnegie – Building Wealth Through Value

Andrew Carnegie, one of history's wealthiest men, did not merely sell steel—he revolutionized an entire industry.

✅ Developed cost-effective, high-quality steel that transformed railroads and skyscrapers.
✅ His innovations propelled industrial growth in America.
✅ Later, he donated much of his wealth, funding libraries, universities, and philanthropic causes.

📖 **Quote from *The Gospel of Wealth* by Carnegie:**
"The man who dies rich, dies disgraced."

🔹 **Lesson:** The greatest wealth builders think beyond money—they focus on impact and legacy.

6. Reference to My Book – The Role of Value in Wealth Creation

📖 **From *The Unstoppable Road to Wealth Creation***
In my book, I emphasize that sustainable wealth stems from consistent value creation.

✅ The wealthy prioritize problem-solving over wealth accumulation.
✅ Your earning potential is directly linked to the impact you create.

🔹 **Lesson:** If you chase money, success is uncertain. If you create value, wealth will follow effortlessly.

Conclusion: Become a Person of Value, and Wealth Will Follow

📖 **Final Quote:**
"Strive not to be a success, but rather to be of value." — Albert Einstein

💡 **Key Takeaways:**
✅ Wealthy individuals focus on solving big problems, not merely making money.
✅ Value creation can take many forms, from innovation to education.
✅ The greater the value you provide, the greater your financial rewards.
✅ Shifting your mindset from income to impact is the key to lasting success.

🚀 **Final Lesson:** Wealth is not about how much money you make—it's about how much value you bring to the world. If you commit to becoming a person of extraordinary value, financial success will naturally follow.

CHAPTER 23: THE ART OF DECISION-MAKING – HOW THE WEALTHY MAKE BOLD AND SMART CHOICES

Introduction

"In moments of decision, the best thing you can do is the right choice, the next best is the wrong one, and the worst is doing nothing." — Theodore Roosevelt

A key characteristic of the ultra-wealthy is their ability to make firm, strategic, and bold choices. While the average person hesitates, overanalyses, or avoids risk, the wealthy make calculated moves that put them ahead.

This chapter will cover:
✅ How wealthy individuals approach decision-making.

✅ Methods to make faster and more effective choices.
✅ The role of logic, intuition, and risk evaluation in financial success.
✅ Historical and modern case studies of decisive wealth-building choices.
✅ Practical techniques to enhance your decision-making abilities.

---

1. The Wealthy Recognize the Impact of Decisions

📖 *"Successful individuals make decisions quickly and change them slowly. Unsuccessful individuals do the opposite."* — Napoleon Hill, *Think and Grow Rich*

Wealthy individuals understand that every decision they make has a lasting financial impact. Instead of being paralyzed by fear or doubt, they develop confidence in making informed, timely choices.

How Decision-Making Differs Between the Wealthy and the Poor

🚫 Poor Decision-Making:
❌ Overanalyses every possibility.
❌ Fears making mistakes.
❌ Postpones opportunities due to uncertainty.
❌ Avoids risks altogether.

✅ Wealthy Decision-Making:
✔ Collects key information quickly.
✔ Takes strategic risks.
✔ Learns from setbacks rather than fearing them.
✔ Focuses on long-term gains over short-term fears.

Example: Jeff Bezos and the 'Regret Minimization Framework'

✅ Bezos left his stable job to launch Amazon.

✅ He asked himself: *"Will I regret not doing this when I'm 80?"*

✅ His answer was yes, so he made the bold move.

✅ That one decision led to one of the most valuable companies in history.

🔹 *Lesson:* Avoiding decisions out of fear of failure can mean missing the greatest opportunities of your life.

2. The Wealthy Weigh Risk and Reward

📖 *"The biggest risk is avoiding all risks."* — Mark Zuckerberg

Rather than avoiding risk, the ultra-wealthy analyze and manage it effectively. They recognize that high rewards often come with some degree of uncertainty.

How Wealthy Individuals Assess Risk vs. Reward:

🔹 **Step 1:** Identify the opportunity—What are the potential gains?

🔹 **Step 2:** Assess the worst-case scenario—What could go wrong?

🔹 **Step 3:** Evaluate the likelihood of success—Are the odds favorable?

🔹 **Step 4:** Take action if the potential reward outweighs the risk.

Example: Elon Musk's All-In Bet on Tesla and SpaceX

✅ Musk invested everything into Tesla and SpaceX.

✅ He faced possible bankruptcy but remained committed to long-term innovation.

✅ Both companies are now industry leaders worth billions.

🔹 **Lesson:** The wealthy take intelligent risks—they don't gamble recklessly, but they also don't avoid opportunities out of fear.

3. The 5-Second Rule for Swift and Smart Decision-Making

📖 *"If you have a good idea, act on it. Procrastination kills more dreams than failure ever will."* — Tony Robbins

One of the major barriers to wealth creation is indecision. The longer you delay making a choice, the harder it becomes to take action.

The 5-Second Rule by Mel Robbins

🚀 When you feel the urge to act on a goal, count down from 5-4-3-2-1 and move forward immediately.

✅ This method helps eliminate hesitation.

✅ It prevents overthinking and forces action.

✅ Many successful entrepreneurs use it to break through decision paralysis.

Personal Story: Applying the 5-Second Rule to Grow My Business

Early on, I hesitated on a major business expansion opportunity due to fear of failure. But after implementing the 5-second rule, I decided to take the leap.

✅ That single decision led to immense business growth.

✅ Had I waited, I would have missed a life-changing opportunity.

🔹 *Lesson:* Quick decision-making leads to faster progress.

4. Historical Case Study: Andrew Carnegie's Bold Business Leap

Andrew Carnegie became one of the wealthiest men in history by making bold, strategic choices.

✅ He identified the steel industry as a major opportunity.

✅ Despite having no prior experience in steel, he invested heavily.

✅ That decision led to the creation of Carnegie Steel, making him one of the richest individuals of his era.

📖 *"Do not seek approval—only the satisfaction of knowing you did your best."* — Andrew Carnegie

◆ *Lesson:* Wealthy individuals do not wait for absolute certainty—they take calculated leaps of faith.

5. Practical Exercises to Strengthen Your Decision-Making Abilities

📖 *"The way to get started is to quit talking and begin doing."* — Walt Disney

If making confident choices is a struggle, try these practical exercises:

Exercise 1: The 2-Minute Rule

◆ When faced with a minor decision, allow yourself no more than two minutes to decide.

◆ This prevents analysis paralysis.

Exercise 2: Worst-Case Scenario Planning

◆ Write down the worst possible outcome of a decision.

◆ Ask: *"Can I handle this?"* If the answer is yes, proceed.

Exercise 3: The 'Yes' Challenge

◆ For the next seven days, commit to saying *yes* to at least one new opportunity per day.

◆ This builds decision-making confidence and pushes you beyond your comfort zone.

◆ *Lesson:* The more you practice making decisions, the better you become.

6. Reference to My Book – The Influence of Bold Choices in Wealth Creation

📖 *From* The Unstoppable Road to Wealth Creation

In my book, I highlight how every wealthy entrepreneur and investor has had to make crucial, life-altering decisions.
✅ The skill of making timely, informed choices is essential for building wealth.
✅ Indecision is one of the greatest obstacles to success.
✅ The ability to take smart risks distinguishes the wealthy from the average.

Conclusion: Take Charge of Your Choices, Take Charge of Your Wealth

📖 *"Successful individuals don't fear making decisions—they fear not making them."* — Grant Cardone

💡 Key Takeaways:

✔ Decision-making drives financial success.
✔ The wealthy make strategic moves rather than waiting for certainty.
✔ Taking action—no matter how small—is always better than inaction.
✔ Your financial future is shaped by the choices you make today.
🚀 Start making bold, informed decisions now, and take control of your wealth journey!

--------BONUS CHAPTERS--------

CHAPTER 24: THE WEALTH BLUEPRINT – TURNING KNOWLEDGE INTO ACTION

Introduction:

Knowledge is Only Powerful When Applied

"Knowledge is not power until it is applied." — Dale Carnegie
After delving into the habits, mindset, strategies, and secrets of the wealthy, the key question remains: How will you use this knowledge?

Understanding wealth creation is only valuable when followed by action. Many people read books, attend seminars, and absorb knowledge but fail to implement it. The truly wealthy don't just dream—they take action and execute plans.

This final chapter is designed to help you create your own wealth-building roadmap—a structured approach to transforming insights from this book into real financial success.

---

1. Why People Struggle to Take Action on Wealth Building

🕮 *Quote:*
"Vision without execution is hallucination." — Thomas Edison
The primary difference between the wealthy and those who struggle financially is not intelligence, luck, or background—it's execution. Many people have great ideas and knowledge but fail to take the first step.

Common Barriers to Action:

⊘ Fear of failure – "What if I lose money?"
⊘ Perfectionism – "I need to know everything before starting."
⊘ Lack of urgency – "I'll begin next year."
⊘ Overanalysing – "What's the best investment strategy?"

✓ Wealthy individuals overcome these obstacles and take action regardless of uncertainties.
◆ **Key Lesson***:* Success isn't about avoiding failure—it's about learning, adapting, and persisting.

2. Designing Your Wealth Blueprint – A Practical Guide

📖 *Quote:*
"Don't just read this book. Do something. Take action. Live your dreams." — Grant Cardone

Step 1: Define Your Wealth Vision

🔹 What does financial success mean to you?
🔹 How much wealth do you want to accumulate in 5, 10, or 20 years?
🔹 What investment or business strategies align with your goals?
✅ Clearly define and document your financial goals.

Step 2: Select Your Wealth-Building Channels

Wealth is generated through multiple streams of income. Choose the ones that match your skills and interests:
💰 **Entrepreneurship** – Launch a business or side hustle.
📈 **Investing** – Stocks, real estate, commodities, or cryptocurrency.
🏦 **Assets** – Create passive income sources like rental properties or dividend investments.
✅ Choose at least one path and take immediate action.

Step 3: Develop the Right Mindset and Habits

Success is 80% mindset and 20% strategy. A strong mentality sustains long-term financial growth.

❢ Daily Wealth-Building Habits:

✅ Read books on finance and successful entrepreneurs.
✅ Build relationships with successful, wealth-oriented individuals.
✅ Monitor and manage your income, expenses, and investments.
✅ Keep learning, adapting, and growing financially.

Step 4: Take Decisive, Consistent Action

📖 *Quote:*
"The secret of getting ahead is getting started." — Mark Twain
🔥 The biggest mistake is waiting for the perfect opportunity. Start small but start now:
✔ Buy your first stock or asset.
✔ Launch your business idea.
✔ Establish a disciplined saving and investing routine.
✔ Make wise financial choices daily.
✅ Action trumps perfection—just begin.

---

3. Overcoming Setbacks – The Wealthy Never Quit

📖 *Quote:*
"Success is going from failure to failure without losing enthusiasm." — Winston Churchill
Every wealthy individual has faced failures, financial losses, and obstacles. The difference? They refuse to quit.

🔹 Example: Walt Disney was fired from his first job for "lacking creativity." He went bankrupt before founding Disney.
🔹 Example: Henry Ford failed five times before pioneering the automobile industry.
🔹 Example: Oprah Winfrey was once deemed "unfit for television"

before becoming a billionaire.

✅ Failure is not the opposite of success—it is part of the journey.

---

4. Wealth is a Continuous Journey – A Reference to My Previous Book

📖 *From The Unstoppable Road to Wealth Creation*

Wealth-building is an ongoing commitment. It requires:

✔ Continuous learning and self-improvement.

✔ Adapting to financial shifts and trends.

✔ Building resilience and determination.

✔ Maintaining focus on long-term prosperity.

🔹 ***Key Takeaway:*** Wealth creation is a marathon, not a sprint—consistency is everything.

---

5. Your 90-Day Wealth Action Plan – A Final Challenge

📖 *Quote:*

"The best time to plant a tree was 20 years ago. The second best time is now." — Chinese Proverb

To ensure you take action, follow this structured 90-day challenge:

🚀 Weeks 1-4:

🔹 Set specific financial goals.

🔹 Choose a primary wealth-building step (business, investment, savings).

🔹 Start tracking your financial progress.

🚀 Weeks 5-8:

◆ Study and make your first investment.

◆ Establish a daily financial growth habit.

◆ Expand your network—connect with successful individuals.

🚀 Weeks 9-12:

◆ Evaluate your progress and adjust strategies.

◆ Refine your financial plan for continued success.

◆ Commit to long-term financial independence.

✅ By the end of 90 days, you will have made more progress than most people make in a lifetime.

Conclusion: Wealth is in Your Hands

📖 *Final Quote:*
"What you do today determines your wealth tomorrow." — Robert Kiyosaki
The final takeaway from this book is simple: Your financial destiny is in your hands. The wealthy are not merely lucky—they take deliberate actions to build lasting wealth.

💡 Key Lessons to Remember:

✔ Knowledge without action is meaningless.

✔ Wealth is built through daily, intentional choices.

✔ Failure is a stepping stone—never let setbacks stop you.

✔ The best time to start is **NOW.**

🚀 Your wealth-building journey begins today. Take action, make bold moves, and create your financial legacy.

------FINAL CHAPTER-------

CHAPTER 25: THE WEALTHY LIVE WITH PURPOSE AND INTENTION

Introduction:

Wealth is a Continuous Journey

"Wealth is not merely about money; it represents freedom, influence, and legacy." — Justine Ehiwario.
As we reach the end of this book, it's important to remember that wealth isn't a fixed destination—it's an ongoing journey of learning, evolving, and applying financial wisdom.

Wealthy individuals don't accumulate money just for its sake; they see it as a tool for securing freedom, unlocking opportunities, and leaving a meaningful impact. Their focus is on constructing a lasting legacy that transcends their lifetime.

Now, the critical question remains: How will you apply this knowledge to your financial future?

---

1. The Key Distinction Between the Wealthy and the Average Person

The primary difference between those who build wealth and those who don't lies not just in what they know but in how consistently they act upon that knowledge.

📖 *Final Quote:*
"The rich invest in time, the poor invest in money." — Warren Buffett

What Wealthy Individuals Do:

✅ Take calculated financial risks
✅ Implement long-term wealth strategies
✅ Commit to continuous learning and adaptability
✅ Make their money generate more wealth

What the Average Person Does:

⊘ Avoids financial risks out of fear
⊘ Spends more than they invest
⊘ Relies solely on a single income source
⊘ Remains trapped in the cycle of financial struggle

💡 **Final Lesson:** The financial choices and habits you establish today will shape your future wealth.

---

2. Next Steps: Turning Knowledge into Action

🕮 *Quote:*
"Your future is created by what you do today, not tomorrow." — Robert Kiyosaki

Reading this book has given you a solid framework, but knowledge alone won't bring wealth—action will.

Steps to Start Building Wealth:

✅ **Act Now** – The best time to start was yesterday; the second-best time is today.
✅ **Apply One Principle at a Time** – Avoid feeling overwhelmed; take small, steady steps toward success.
✅ **Develop Daily Wealth Habits** – Make reading, learning, and investing a part of your routine.
✅ **Adopt a Long-Term Perspective** – Wealth accumulation is a marathon, not a sprint.
✅ **Surround Yourself with Wealth-Building Minds** – Your financial network influences your net worth.

🔹 **Challenge:** What step will you take today to move toward financial freedom? Write it down and take action immediately.

---

3. The Final Principle: Creating a Lasting Legacy

🕮 *Quote:*
"A wise man leaves an inheritance to his children's children." — Proverbs 13:22

True wealth creation goes beyond personal success—it's about ensuring future generations benefit from your efforts. The most prosperous families in history didn't just amass wealth; they structured it to endure for centuries.

✅ Educate your family on financial literacy
✅ Establish sustainable wealth-building systems (businesses, investments, real estate)
✅ Use your financial resources to drive positive change in the world

🔹 **Final Lesson:** Wealth is meaningless if it doesn't leave a positive, lasting impact.

---

4. Continuing the Journey: A Reference to My Previous Book

📖 *From The Unstoppable Road to Wealth Creation*

Building wealth demands discipline, patience, and consistency. In *The Unstoppable Road to Wealth Creation*, I laid the foundation for long-term financial success. This book expands on those principles, providing a deeper understanding of how to sustain and grow wealth.

💡 **Final Thought:** Never stop learning, evolving, and improving your financial knowledge. Wealth-building is a lifelong process.

---

5. The Final Challenge: Will You Take Control of Your Financial Future?

📖 *Quote:*
"The only limits to wealth are the ones you place on yourself." — Justine Ehiwario

This is more than just the conclusion of a book—it's the beginning of your wealth journey.

🚀 Will you commit to building financial freedom, or will you let this knowledge fade away without action?

💡 *Make Your Decision Today:*
✓ Take intentional steps toward financial growth
✓ Invest in your financial education
✓ Develop and execute a wealth-building plan
✓ Stay disciplined and persistent in your pursuit

✅ You have all the tools you need—now it's time to create wealth!

Wealth is Yours to Build

💡 Final Thought:

"Wealth is not reserved for a select few. It is created by those who take bold action, remain steadfast, and commit to financial discipline. The choice is yours." — Justine Ehiwario

🌟 Thank you for embarking on this journey through *The Things Wealthy People Do*. I hope it has inspired you to take charge of your financial future and build a life of abundance, success, and lasting impact. 🌟

Final Note to My Readers

Dear Reader,

First and foremost, **thank you** for taking the time to read *The Things Wealthy People Do.* Writing this book has been a deeply personal journey—one filled with reflection, research, and the unwavering desire to share life-changing principles of wealth creation.

If there's one thing I want you to take away from this book, it is this:

💡 Wealth is a mindset before it is money.

It is not about luck, background, or where you started in life. It is about what you **choose to do today** that will shape your financial future. The ultra-wealthy do not rely on chance; they apply principles, take action, and remain committed to their vision, even when challenges arise.

🚀 Your Journey Starts Now!

You now possess the knowledge that has created and sustained wealth for generations. But knowledge alone is **not enough**—it is **action** that separates those who dream of wealth from those who attain it.

✨ **Start where you are.** No matter your current financial situation, begin applying these principles today.
✨ **Stay consistent.** Wealth is built through habits, not occasional effort.
✨ **Keep learning.** The most successful people never stop growing.
✨ **Give back.** True wealth is not just about accumulation but also

about **impact.**

I challenge you to take the lessons from this book and apply them in your life. **One year from now, you should not be in the same financial position you are today.**

💬 Stay Connected!

I would love to hear about your journey—your successes, challenges, and breakthroughs. Feel free to reach out, share your experiences, and stay connected with me through my various platforms.

📨 **Email:** [info@justechinternational.com]
🌍 **Website:** [www.justechinternational.com]

📍 *Remember: The key to wealth is not just in knowing what to do, but in actually doing it.* Take action. Stay disciplined. Build your legacy.

To your financial freedom and success,

– Justine Ehiwario

Acknowledgments

Writing *The Things Wealthy People Do* has been a journey of passion, research, and personal reflection. This book would not have been possible without the invaluable lessons from mentors, financial experts, historical figures, and personal experiences that have shaped my understanding of wealth creation.

A Special Thank You To:

My Family – My wife, Odion, and my children, Justine, Jason, and Jolene. Your love, support, and encouragement are the foundation of everything I do. You are my greatest inspiration, and I hope this book serves as a legacy of knowledge for you and future generations.

My Closest Brother, Michael – Thank you for being a constant source of wisdom, motivation, and encouragement. Your insights and support have been instrumental in this journey.

My Readers – To every reader who has picked up this book: Thank you for investing in your financial future. Your success is the reason this book was written.

My Mentors and Influences – From historical figures to modern financial experts, your work and teachings have inspired me to research, learn, and apply the principles of wealth creation.

My Supporters and Business Partners – To my business networks, colleagues, and those who have supported *Jay T Solutions Ltd*, *Jay T Clothing*, *Justech International*, *Jay T Solutions-Engineering Services*, *Jay T luxury Homes*, *Jay T Prime Properties*, and my other ventures—your belief in my vision has been priceless.

This book is a testament to the fact that **wealth is within reach for anyone willing to learn, take action, and stay disciplined.** Thank you all for being part of this journey!

Recommended Reading List

To further your knowledge on wealth-building, mindset, and financial mastery, I recommend the following books:

My Other Book:

🕮 *The Unstoppable Road to Wealth Creation* – Justine Ehiwario

This book expands on many of the ideas discussed in *The Things Wealthy People Do*, providing a deeper look into strategies for achieving financial success. I encourage you to read it for further insights.

Classic Wealth-Building Books:

🕮 *Think and Grow Rich* – Napoleon Hill

🕮 *The Science of Getting Rich* – Wallace D. Wattles

🕮 *The Art of Money Getting* – P.T. Barnum

🕮 *Rich Dad Poor Dad* – Robert Kiyosaki

🕮 *The Richest Man in Babylon* – George S. Clason

Modern Financial & Business Books:

🕮 *The Millionaire Fast lane* – MJ DeMarco

🕮 *The Psychology of Money* – Morgan Housel

🕮 *The 48 Laws of Power* – Robert Greene

🕮 *Unshakeable* – Tony Robbins

🕮 *The Wealth Choice: Success Secrets of Black Millionaires* – Dr. Dennis Kimbro

Books on Investing & Financial Literacy:

🕮 *The Intelligent Investor* – Benjamin Graham

🕮 *Your Money or Your Life* – Vicki Robin & Joe Dominguez

🕮 *I Will Teach You to Be Rich* – Ramit Sethi

🕮 *Secrets of the Millionaire Mind* – T. Harv Eker

Inspirational & Mindset Books:

🕮 *The Power of Your Subconscious Mind* – Joseph Murphy

🕮 *Atomic Habits* – James Clear

🕮 *The 10X Rule* – Grant Cardone

🕮 *You Are a Badass at Making Money* – Jen Sincero

Final Words

✸ *You now have the knowledge. What you do next is entirely up to you.* ✸

Wealth is not reserved for a select few—it is created through intentional decisions, discipline, and taking action. Go forth, apply what you have learned, and build the financial future you deserve.

🚀 Your journey to wealth starts now!

Thank you for being part of this journey. I wish you success, financial freedom, and an extraordinary life!

– Justine Ehiwario

THE END!

www.ingramcontent.com/pod-product-compliance
Lightning Source LLC
LaVergne TN
LVHW050544160826
845677LV00011B/2169

* 9 7 8 3 2 8 1 7 4 1 9 3 0 *